D1616969

UNCANNY SUBJECTS

UNCANNY SUBJECTS

Aging in Contemporary Narrative

AMELIA DeFALCO

THE OHIO STATE UNIVERSITY PRESS · COLUMBUS

Library of Congress Cataloging-in-Publication Data
DeFalco, Amelia, 1978–
Uncanny subjects : aging in contemporary narrative / Amelia DeFalco.
p. cm.
Includes bibliographical references and index.
ISBN 978-0-8142-1113-7 (cloth : alk. paper)—ISBN 978-0-8142-9211-2 (cd-rom) 1. Old
age in literature. 2. Identity (Psychology) in old age. 3. Aging in literature. 4. Aging in
motion pictures. I. Title.
PN56.04D44 2010
809.'93354—dc22
2009037117

This book is available in the following editions:
Cloth (ISBN 978-0-8142-1113-7)
CD-ROM (ISBN 978-0-8142-9211-2)

Cover illustration: John W. Ford, *Forgotten Space: Pink Wall and Trees*. Archival Digital
Print, A/P, 8" x 16", 2008. Gallery Representation: transit gallery, Hamilton, Ontario,
Canada.

Cover design by Melissa Ryan
Text design by Juliet Williams
Type set in Adobe Sabon
Printed by Thomson-Shore, Inc.

♾ The paper used in this publication meets the minimum requirements of the American
National Standard for Information Sciences—Permanence of Paper for Printed Library
Materials. ANSI Z39.48–1992.

9 8 7 6 5 4 3 2 1

For R.H.
And for Irene
With love and gratitude

CONTENTS

PREFACE

IN THE SUMMER of 2005 I had dinner with my grandparents at a restaurant near their home in Utica, New York. The restaurant was chosen because it was my grandmother's favorite, or more precisely, it was the only place outside her home where she would willingly eat a meal. Our server, a woman I'd guess to be in her fifties, was friendly, in a somewhat overbearing way. She took a self-conscious liking to my grandmother and repeatedly commented on her looks and demeanor to the rest of us at the table, including my grandfather and my parents. My grandmother had lost most of her hearing and was beginning to have trouble with her memory as a result of Alzheimer's. Her strategy, devised over a decade ago when her hearing began to fail, was to smile or even laugh gently when people spoke to her, which we had to come to recognize as her response to inquiries she could not hear. "Is it just her hearing or is anything else wrong with her?" the server asked us at one point. And then later, in reference to my grandmother's long gray hair, which was pinned to the back of her head with a great number of bobby pins, "most ladies cut and dye and curl their hair into these big poufs, her long hair is so cute, she's just so *cute*." My grandmother continued to smile.

This encounter, which occurred around the same time I was embarking on this study of aging, proved instructive. The woman's remarks had much to say about the difference age makes. Her comments reflect the kind of pathologization and objectification that culture inflicts on old age, a pattern of othering that can at least partly explain the antipathy felt by many at the prospect of being categorized as "old." Such a category, as the server's comments illustrate, can render one invisible or entirely absent; although present, my grandmother was transformed into the third person. The aging, or here aged, subject is both objectified and exiled. The woman's observations reveal her efforts to read correctly the sign of difference that sat before her. This study seeks to restore what this kind of quotidian interaction erases—the *presence* of an older subject—and, more importantly, to investigate the repercussions of occupying the tenuous cultural position of "old."

Though old age may be a category that awaits everyone lucky enough to live a long life, experiences of the difference of age vary immensely as aging interacts with other cultural categories including race, class, ethnicity, and, most dramatically, gender. As feminism has made clear, gender is largely responsible for the formation of subjectivity, and one need only glance at any representation within popular media, whether print, television, or digital, to quickly recognize that aging is distinctly gendered. Casually surveying the anti-aging discourse of magazines displayed at the supermarket checkout, billboards, "makeover" reality-TV shows, and other so-called women's television programming, one might be tempted to assume that aging is primarily a "woman's issue." Indeed, the server's comments touched only my grandmother, though my grandfather, who is actually one year older, was also at the table. Her reference to my grandmother's "cuteness" highlights the role of the "the body as the dominant signifier of old age" and the infantilizing attention paid to "unusual" old bodies (Woodward, *Discontents* 10). The server's remarks draw attention to the either/or logic that forces an old person, or, more precisely, an old woman, into a dilemma: conceal, modify, deny your old age and you may be seen as ridiculous, even slightly shameful; wear your age without adjustment and you are "cute"—innocuous and childish.[1] And yet with-

---

1. Herbert Blau draws attention to the rejection in western culture of bodily adornments in old age, arguing that such attention to appearance points to the existence of desire in the old, a desire that the not-yet-old wish to deny (20). As well, Kathleen Woodward responds to the dilemma between the modification and acceptance of old age in her treatment of cosmetic surgery, arguing that such procedures are meant to resolve this dilemma through invisible correction: "With cosmetic surgery, the mask of the aging body is doubled over. The surface of the body is cut and stretched to disguise the surface of the body. Unlike the hysterical body whose surface is inscribed with symptoms, the objective of the surgically youthful body is to speak nothing" (*Discontents* 162). These issues of concealment and revelation, the visible and invisible, are

out the concealment of cosmetics, dyes, clothing, even surgeries, without appropriate adjustments in activity and behavior made to hide what the not-yet-old, the not-yet-aged, largely interpret as a process of decline and degeneration, the old female subject is rendered benign in other ways, in this case through infantilization.

But I must complicate such a pat gender analysis with a caveat: my grandmother's disability was apparent at the time—the server was warned of her hearing loss, and my grandmother often looked wary or confused. I argue that the intertwining of pathologization and infantilization implied by the woman's comments, which were undoubtedly offered in a spirit of friendly concern, reflects attitudes toward old age and disability as much as gender. Anyone who has spent time in a later-life care facility knows that pathologization, infantilization, and objectification are not reserved for older women alone. In advanced age, men are often deemed "cute" as well. I have no doubt that aging is always inflected by other categories of difference, but my aim is to treat aging as its own difference, which means considering both women *and* men as aging subjects. As a result, discussions of gender have fluctuating prominence throughout my analysis of aging, often implied in the background, and occasionally coming into sharp focus, as in chapter 3. My interests lie in the meanings that arise from the often disorienting and inevitable changes of age, as well as how such changes are revised and rewritten by gender. Gender and age are deeply entwined, but I argue that the difference enacted by old age sometimes outweighs the concerns of gender. Meeting a retired elderly professor and department chair at a party he attended with his daughter, I was reminded of my grandmother's enforced invisibility. The man's daughter explained how she is consistently relegated to the role of interpreter when they are together, though her father suffers no cognitive disabilities. Strangers often spoke of her father in the third person when he stood or sat right beside her. Such interactions reveal how people in contemporary western culture repeatedly interpret the bodily signs of advanced age as indicators of reduced agency and comprehension.

Between the generation of the retired professor and my grandmother and my own generation is a demographic anomaly. Because of the combination of increased life expectancy and lower birth rates, the aging baby boom has produced an unusually large segment of the population approaching retirement and later life: "In 2001, one in every eight Americans was over the age of 65; in 2030 one in four people will be over the age of 65" (Mooney, Knox, and Schacht 277). Throughout the western world,

---

integral to the exploration of images and doubling presented in chapter 3.

educational institutions, governmental bodies, and marketers are responding to the demographic phenomenon captured in the title of Kausler and
Kausler's encyclopedia of aging: *The Graying of America* (2001), now in
its second edition. Of course the United States is not the only country with
an aging population; demographic shifts are happening all over the indus-
trialized world, as Laura Katz Olson points out in her introduction to *The
Graying of the World: Who Will Care for the Frail Elderly?* (1). The anxious question of Olson's title tellingly constructs older subjects as a feeble,
helpless population, a looming burden. The worried title underlines a central feature of demographic analysis and projection: fear that an excessive
number of old people will produce a destructively imbalanced society. But
aging anxieties are not limited to a fear of old age as a faceless mass of
others. The popular media effectively capitalize on the public's angst-rid-
den awareness of aging *within*, a frightening otherness that consumers are
encouraged to repress at all costs. As larger and larger market segments
recognize the specter of the "frail elderly" in their own futures and reflections, an anti-aging industry (products, services, and the companies who
promote them) has become increasingly powerful, not to mention lucrative. The us/them division declared in a title such as Olson's cannot hold:
the audience it addresses, the not-yet-old, not-yet-frail, can only deny and
objectify old age for so long before its familiarity becomes undeniable and
protective categories begin to crumble.

Nonetheless, many aging subjects struggle to delay the looming
"frailty" of later life in a variety of ways. As more and more consumers
age into old age, products and services emerge from the expanding anti-
aging industry with the ostensible goal of easing the "burden" of aging.
Recently in North America and the United Kingdom, numerous education
and research facilities have developed to study the increasingly pertinent
subject of human aging. Such institutes operate in Newcastle, Sheffield,
Oxford, and at the universities of Toronto, North Carolina, and Pennsylvania, to name just a few. In 1996 the Buck Institute, "the first independent research facility in the country [United States] focused solely on
aging and age-related disease," opened its doors in Novato, California
("About the Institute"). The year 1993 saw the inception of the American
Academy of Anti-Aging Medicine, or A4M, which proclaims "anti-aging
medicine . . . as the new health care paradigm" and offers "a solution to
alleviate some of the burden of this burgeoning older population" ("What
Is Anti-Aging Medicine?"). The aims of these institutions dovetail neatly
with popular media representational practices, in which aging functions
as a dangerous villain that must be battled at every opportunity, with the

various providers of anti-aging products and services promising effective weapons of defense. As declared on the A4M Web site, "America is being summoned to a new call to arms" ("What Is Anti-Aging Medicine?").

Aging and its anxieties have also gained prominence in television programming. In reality-TV shows such as *Age of Love* and *Ten Years Younger* (with UK and U.S. versions), age produces the central conflict. In the former, female contestants in their twenties ("kittens") and their forties ("cougars") compete for the attention of an eligible bachelor. In *Ten Years Younger,* contestants, who include a few token males, are judged by strangers who guess their ages, setting the figure that specialists in hair, makeup, and (in the UK version only) cosmetic surgery attempt to decrease by ten years. All three shows have appeared within the past few years. It seems age has become the new, trendy difference in reality television—such shows have long capitalized on gender, race, and class—that can effectively triangulate familiar gender binaries, as in *Age of Love.* Old age has long been a subject of fear and trepidation, even disgust,[2] but these anxieties are taking on a new pitch in a time of rapidly aging populations. My project is an attempt to address the imbalance between the preoccupation with age in popular and scientific culture and the near invisibility of age as a category of difference in humanities scholarship.

Contemporary social contexts provide multiple narratives of aging, in various media, that rely on numeric boundaries to mitigate the anxieties surrounding aging into old age. A case in point appears in a letter from the editor of the newly launched Canadian edition of *More* magazine, "Canada's magazine celebrating women over 40" (Summer 2007). In response to a sixty-nine-year-old reader who urged the magazine not to "forget those of us who are over 60" (Taylor), the editor explained that "our primary focus is communicating with women in their forties and fifties," though she implored the marginalized sixty-nine-year-old to "continue to read and enjoy *More*" ("Editor's Note"). The magazine aimed at older women makes efforts to exclude the old and thereby protect its target audience from age by association. But in spite of all such efforts to segment aging into discrete periods, and categories, we are all growing older every moment, and this constant movement of time will eventually undermine any attempt to fix age identity.

The movement of aging is the movement of our lives, and this dynamism aligns aging with narrative: both are a function of time, of change, of

---

2. For historical accounts of the marginalization of the elderly, see Achenbaum, Beauvoir, Demos, Katz, Laslett, Mangum, Small.

one thing happening after another. Human lives follow a certain biological narrative trajectory that moves from birth through maturity into adulthood and old age toward death. As a result, subjects understand their lives through narrative trajectories—through stories—not necessarily as they are living moment to moment, but in reflection, reflection that becomes, many argue, more and more likely as one ages into old age (see, for example, Butler; Woodward, "Telling Stories"). For these reasons, I found that my study of aging quickly became an inquiry into narrative and its relation to the construction and comprehension of selves.

The narrativity of aging inspired me to look to storytellers to better understand the difference of age. I discovered that literature and film have much to contribute to the discourse of aging identity and its various anxieties. I have chosen to focus on fictional accounts of aging into old age because life writing about aging has been theorized more frequently and fully already, but also because I was interested in authors and filmmakers as theorists of sorts; I looked to see how they *imagined* aging. As I read fiction and watched films, I recognized a recurring depiction of aging into old age as a disorienting process of self-estrangement, one that often shed light on the strange nature of temporal identity. In short, these texts exposed a version of what Freud called the "uncanny," which I reconfigure as the uncanniness of aging. My own theorization of difference and identity is a response to a perceived thematic similitude within contemporary narratives of aging. To that end, I have focused my discussion on a small number of texts that have, each in its own way, taught me something specific about the implications of uncanny aging in the late twentieth and early twenty-first centuries, about the difficulty of reconciling the conflicting versions of identity that culture offers its subjects. My own theorizing is an attempt to better understand the implications of these narratives.

In addressing the uncanniness of aging I am not entirely alone. My work builds on the pioneers of critical aging studies—in particular, Simone de Beauvoir and Kathleen Woodward, both of whom address the strange otherness of old age. In her brief but astute characterization of old age as the "Other within" (320), Beauvoir evokes the dialectic of repression and recognition that makes aging so disturbing and, I argue, uncanny. My project engages theories of aging and identity posited in theory *and* fiction. Beauvoir's description of the vertiginous effect of aging is echoed in fictional depictions of aging into old age as an unsettling discovery of repressed strangeness, calling to mind Freud's account of the uncanny as "that class of the frightening which leads back to what is known of old and long familiar" (340). His essay on the subject has often functioned as a primary text in discussions of literary instability and the inscrutability of meaning (see, for example, Cixous, Kofman, Kristeva, Lydenberg, Royle, Wolfreys). Though Freud's essay is a formative influence on my theorization of uncanny identity, my analysis is not strictly psychoanalytic; those interested in such a reading should consult Kathleen Woodward's fine book *Aging and Its Discontents*. In my own treatment of aging, Freud's essay functions less as a primary text than as an enabling source of provocation, its multiplicity and open-endedness inciting forays into wider-ranging concerns. My treatment of Freud's essay departs from recent theorization of the uncanny, which often analyzes and even dismantles the various sections of Freud's text (see, in particular, Cixous, Lydenberg, Royle); instead, Freud functions as one of many interpretive voices offering insight into the strange otherness of aging.

This study remains an unusual one in the humanities. Despite shifting demographics, age remains an undertheorized site of difference in cultural studies. The most recent edition of Routledge's *The Cultural Studies Reader* makes no mention of age or aging in any of its eleven sections. There are sections devoted to "Ethnicity and Multiculturalism" and "Sexuality and Gender," but for all its attention to the "The New Cultural Politics of Difference," to borrow from the title of Cornel West's essay in the collection, age remains invisible. Similarly, a 448-page reader on identity recently published by Blackwell announces the noteworthy categories of difference in its title: *Identities: Race, Class, Gender and Nationality*. In their representation of the contemporary, anthologies of cultural studies and of critical and literary theory repeatedly overlook the structuring force of what Woodward calls "gerontophobia" (*Discontents* 193) in western culture. But this oversight is limited to the cultural studies work done by scholars in the humanities. Age analysis flourishes in the social sciences. This project is an attempt to build bridges of understanding between these disciplines, and to demonstrate why such interaction might be productive. My perspective emerges from training in literature and cinema studies, and consequently, this project has its roots in literary discourse. Because the field of aging studies has been largely dominated by the social sciences, my literary approach in itself fosters a kind of interdisciplinarity. To that end, I have tried to function as a translator between these often discrete fields of inquiry, to produce a book for a diverse audience, for any reader invested in the theorization of identity. In her landmark study of aging, Woodward remarks, "We repress the subject of aging. We relegate aging to others. We do not recognize it in ourselves" (Woodward, *Discontents* 193). Here Woodward is explaining the operations and effects of western culture's gerontophobia, but I think her remarks also effectively elaborate the critical invisibility of aging in humanities scholarship. This study of aging and identity in fiction and film is a step toward reversing the critical repression of aging, an initial gesture toward revelation and understanding that I hope will soon open into a wider field of study.

I conclude with a final anecdote, this one from the other end of the age continuum. My own relative youth has led many to question my motives for studying old age. "Aging?" my sister-in-law asked in an email, finding such interests unlikely, even bizarre, in someone "so young." This is a common response to descriptions of my work, and I think the recurrence of this question has much to say about the difference of aging. It is not new for scholars of literature and film to explore issues outside their own range of experience; indeed, one of fiction's primary pleasures is its ability to lead its readers and spectators beyond the familiar. And though one's own identity must often be reckoned with when one strays into territories of identity politics different from one's own, there is some consensus that studying the workings of misogyny or racism in a text teaches one about categories of gender and race, about the function of difference. Cultural critics have come to recognize that everyone is implicated; we are all subjects of gender, race, sexuality. Yet aging remains somehow *different,* somehow outside the realm of theories of identity, a different difference, one might say. Denial allows "aging" to remain the concern of the "aged," despite the fact that we are *all* unavoidably implicated in discussions of aging. Like everyone around me, including those who ask "why aging?," I am constantly aging and with luck I will become old. "Why aging?"—I think perhaps the essential question is "why *not* aging?" Why do so few identity theorists enter into these discussions? What is so unsettling about aging, and what is so "different" about old age? It is questions such as these that this study attempts to answer.

DEFINING AGE

MY FOCUS in *Uncanny Subjects* is primarily the condition of "old" age, or more precisely, the experience of aging into old age. Of course "old" is a highly relative term, largely dependent on perspective—hence the common preference for the more transparently comparative term "older." However, governments and institutions frequently erect boundaries based on age in their designation of "seniors" and appropriate, or even mandatory, ages for retirement: typically, the age of sixty-five has been the border used to distinguish between the old and the not-yet-old. I am not so rigid in my categorization. My theorization depends on the relationality of aging, examining fictional subjects who, regardless of actual age, are forced to confront their status as "old." Though many of my observations and arguments regarding age and aging are relevant to the overall process of aging, much of my analysis attends to "older" subjects, since, as I argue, this exaggerated, culturally loaded experience of becoming and being "old" can engender a new perspective on identity. Though the transitions from childhood to adolescence and adolescence to adulthood are clearly aspects of aging, the transition into the category of "old" compels older subjects to consider aging as a process of culturally determined decline.

ACKNOWLEDGMENTS

FIRST, I AM grateful to Linda Hutcheon, whose encouragement and support have made this book possible. From our earliest conversations on the subject, she propelled me forward, inspiring and provoking my research with her astute insights. I was fortunate to a have a number of talented readers comment on earlier versions of the manuscript. In particular, Naomi Morgenstern, Magdalene Redekop, and Catharine Stimpson offered insightful, challenging feedback, which has been enormously helpful. I also wish to acknowledge The Ohio State University Press's anonymous readers whose comments assisted me in my revisions. Thanks to Maggie Diehl, Juliet Williams, and Jennifer Shoffey Forsythe for their careful assembly of words and images. Sandy Crooms at The Ohio State University Press has been a most reassuring guide, ferrying the project through the various stages of publication.

I was fortunate to have expert assistance when it came to the visual aspects of the book. Terry Odette was invaluable for his skill with image capture technology. As well, I am thankful to John Ford for allowing me to use his beautiful, haunting artwork on the book's cover.

For his seemingly inexhaustible encouragement I thank my spouse and constant reader, Robert Hemmings. As patient listener, tireless cheerleader, and sagacious challenger, he helped make both the process and the product feel meaningful and worthwhile. I acknowledge him with deep gratitude and affection.

My family and friends have also contributed to the personal significance of this project. In particular, I want to thank my grandmother, Irene Stevens, whose immense kindness and generosity continued throughout her struggles with Alzheimer's disease. My efforts at interpreting the devastating effects of this illness are the result of my own attachment to one of its many victims. She is sorely missed. My parents and brothers have, as always, nourished me as I worked with good food, good conversation, and good humor. I thank them all for bolstering my spirits when my enthusiasm lagged.

I wish to acknowledge the journal *Canadian Literature*, where a portion of chapter 1 appeared as "'And then—': Narrative Identity and Uncanny Aging in *The Stone Angel*," volume 198, Autumn 2008.

UNCANNY SUBJECTS

> [T]he uncanny is that class of the frightening which leads back to what
> is known of old and long familiar.
>
> —Freud, "The Uncanny" 340

THIS STUDY addresses age as an undertheorized sign of difference in the humanities, a difference that contemporary narrative fiction and film can help illuminate. The twentieth and twenty-first centuries are important times for a reconsideration of aging into old age, given what is sometimes anxiously referred to as the "graying" of North America. The unprecedented rise in older populations in recent years has increased the attention paid to aging and the elderly across a variety of disciplines, including biology, psychology, and sociology. In the United States anti-aging has become a multibillion-dollar industry supported by the American Academy of Anti-Aging Medicine. Efforts to combat the signs of aging have never been stronger, or more lucrative; a cultural obsession with youth eclipses a growing aging population, furthering the contradictory position of the aging subject as culturally masked and erased, sequestered into institutions for the aged, and, at the same time, visibly present and pathologized.

Within both popular and scientific discourses, aging has largely been construed as a process of decline moving toward death.[1] The discipline of

---

1. Sociologist Stephen Katz provides an insightful inquiry into the repercussions of the advent of gerontology in *Disciplining Old Age: The Formation of Gerontological*

aging studies is largely a response to the oppressive negativity of cultural constructions of aging into old age, working to expose the denigration of aging, replacing myth with insight and evidence. Included among these critics are the theorists Stephen Katz terms "critical gerontologists," who take issue with the "scientificity" of gerontology, and "advocate stronger ties to the humanities, endorse reflexive methodologies, historicize ideological attributes of old age, promote radical political engagement, and resignify the aging process as heterogeneous and indeterminate" (4). In this way branches of aging studies have often functioned much like other early investigations into the issue of "difference": like critics of racial, gendered, ethnic, and sexual difference, critics in aging studies have been invested in exposing aging and old age as a cultural construct, interrogating commonsense notions of age as entirely the result of biological processes, as dominated by decline. Aging studies works to reveal how "the aging body is never just a body subjected to the imperatives of cellular and organic decline, for as it moves through life it is continuously being inscribed and reinscribed with cultural meanings" (Featherstone and Wernick 2–3). As a result there is a great deal of criticism that is recuperative, working to dismantle, or at least interrogate, negative stereotypes and imagery surrounding old age, to think beyond the "discourse of senescence" that Katz identifies (40).

Because preoccupation with "the body as the dominant signifier of old age" in traditional gerontology and popular culture continues to support the association of old age with decline and death, many critics make great efforts to present alternative views of old age that cast doubt on the inevitability of decline, or at the very least, scrutinize the term "old age" and its

---

Knowledge. As he makes clear, the emergence of geriatrics and gerontology in the postwar era as means of studying old age has contributed to conflicting discourses of aging as simultaneously normal and pathological. In these fields, old age was studied primarily as a time of life overdetermined by the body and its decline. Katz suggests the more recent development of "critical gerontology" moves away from gerontology's strict focus on the body and its problems to consider in detail the many contexts of aging (historical, social, economic) (*Disciplining* 3–4). Even prior to the emergence of geriatrics and gerontology, "medical research developed what we have called a discourse of senescence: a new organization of associated ideas and practices that captured the aged body" (40). Practitioners regarded the aged body as a particular entity, as a legible system of signification that communicated its inner "states of disorder" (41). Such inner "disorder" was reflected in what was perhaps the most definitive aspect of the aging body, and by implication of the aging person: the aged body as dying (41). This concept continues to influence contemporary estimations of aging and old age, in both gerontological and popular discourses, obscuring the presence of the elderly with anticipation of their future absence.

ideological sources.[2] The work of Margaret Morganroth Gullette has been invaluable in exposing the damaging, pervasive myth of age as inherently and necessarily a process of decline. The very titles of her books invoke the anti-ageist thrust of her argument: *Safe at Last in the Middle Years, Declining to Decline*, and *Aged by Culture*. Her interdisciplinary research shows how everything from literature to museum displays to the fashion industry enforces, and reinforces, "the dominance of decline narrative, early nostalgia, age apprehensiveness, [the] slicing [of] life into mutually hostile stages," all of which represent "crimes against the life course" (*Aged by Culture* 37).[3] Clearly, the highly negative popular discourse of aging is in need of critical dismantling, and texts such as Gullette's are essential for drawing attention to the ramifications of associating aging exclusively with disintegration. Aging studies scholarship has been invaluable in opening up the field of study, but much like early feminist criticism, the work threatens to slip into a dualistic discourse of positive versus negative representation.[4] There is more to culture's construction of the aging process than competing narratives of progress or decline. Each of these evaluative models can easily become a limiting script that erases particularities and ambiguity, producing or reinforcing either/or diagnoses.

The literature and films examined throughout this study dismantle this dichotomization through their continual reliance on contradiction and ambiguity, on simultaneity, and on inconsistency. Fiction allows age to work as both a category of difference and a particular, personal, imagined experience. Moreover, narrative representations have much to offer the theorization of aging and old age, since both narrative and aging rely on, and reflect, the passage of time. The complex interrelation of narrative studies and aging studies informs this project.

Despite ongoing attention to aging in the social sciences, aging con-

2. Much of aging studies criticism works to correct this bias. Most prominent, perhaps, has been the work of Simon Biggs, Mike Featherstone, Margaret Morganroth Gullette, Mike Hepworth, Stephen Katz, and Kathleen Woodward.

3. Gullette's treatment of the "recovery novel" and museum displays appear in *Aged by Culture* (2004), while her discussion of the fashion industry can be found in her article "The Other End of the Fashion Cycle: Practicing Loss, Learning Decline," which appears in the anthology *Figuring Age* (1999).

4. Early feminist film theory is a good example of this critical evolution. The sociological "positive images" criticism of the early 1970s, particularly that of Marjorie Rosen and Molly Haskell, sought to neatly categorize representations of women as positive or negative. Increased attention to medium-specificity in the late seventies, and the growing diversity of critical voices in the eighties, quickly overshadowed the dualistic discourse of image assessment.

tinues to be what Anne Wyatt-Brown calls "a missing category in current literary theory" (Introduction 1). The late twentieth century proved to scholars the necessity of considerations of difference in the study of literature and film, in particular, of the formative structural distinctions between persons that produce us as subjects, namely distinctions of race and ethnicity, gender and sexuality. Yet a degree of blindness to the influence of age, or more particularly, of old age, on subjectivity remains. Although there are many sociological studies of aging and culture,[5] there are few attempts to examine the ways cultural texts, literature and film, construct multiple narratives of aging that intersect and sometimes conflict with existing critical theories of aging. This is what I address in *Uncanny Subjects*.

AGING AND IDENTITY

Old age renders its subjects both invisible and unmistakable; personhood is often cast into doubt, even imagined as entirely erased, while the body marked by age draws the eye and comment. The collision of hyperbolic specularity—the old person as spectacle and specimen—and cultural invisibility is a paradox that informs much of my study of aging. Older subjects are often rejected by the young, but this rejection is not entirely successful, and takes the form of disavowal rather than successful othering. Disavowal, in Freudian terms, is denial that requires constant effort to maintain, resulting in a paradoxically simultaneous awareness and ignorance.[6] This simultaneous belief/nonbelief in one's own participation in aging toward old age results in a rejection of old age that is impossible for the aging subject to maintain.

5. See, for example, the work of Simon Biggs, Mike Featherstone, Margaret Morganroth Gullette, Haim Hazan, Mike Hepworth, Stephen Katz, Sharon Kaufman, and Andrew Wernick.

6. Describing the process of disavowal that precipitates the attachment to a fetish, Freud writes that the patient "has retained that belief, but he has also given it up. In the conflict between the weight of the unwelcome perception and the force of his counter-wish, a compromise has been reached, as is only possible under the dominance of the unconscious laws of thought—the primary process" ("Fetishism" 353). In Freud's argument this concurrent belief/nonbelief results in a process of substitution, a psychological overinvestment that he terms "fetishism." I cite Freud because disavowal, in this general sense, is crucial to my concept of old age in contemporary culture. The specifics of Freud's argument—the fetish involves a woman's possession of a phallus and subsequent castration—is part of his androcentric legacy, which I seek to destabilize in my own gender analysis.

The disavowal of old age occurs for a number of reasons, all of which rest on the problem of temporality, that is, on the endlessly shifting condition of age. Obviously age (youth, middle age, old age) is an inherently unstable category. In some sense it does not exist since our age identity is always in process. As Simone de Beauvoir explains in her own study of old age, "life is an unstable system in which balance is continually lost and continually recovered: it is inertia that is synonymous with death. Change is the law of life" (17), and it is this constant transformation that gives the concept of age its chimerical quality. It is endlessly slippery, dominated by the ephemerality of time; to speak or write of age is to speak of the present, the constantly receding "now." Because of this obvious fact—aging is a process, not a state—the discourse of aging is endlessly fraught. Until death clicks the stopwatch, one is always aging; how is one to write of old age if one can always be older? This status of age and old age as endlessly shifting works in tandem with the universality of age to undermine efforts to construct age as a category of difference. The tension between universal mutability and the desire for fixed age identities is an important feature of my study.

For many aging becomes a process of alienation, producing a doubling of self that I examine in chapter 3.[7] Joseph Esposito anticipates such a process of estrangement in his appeal to aging as "a new identity crisis" that is "not the crisis of youthful development in which we ask "What will I be like when I am grown up?" but a crisis in which we wonder "Will I still be myself when I have grown old?" (2). Simone de Beauvoir explores the idea in psychoanalytic terms, suggesting that old age is an internalization of difference, of the difference that the old subject comes to represent for the outside world: "Within me it is the Other—that is to say the person I am for the outsider—who is old: and that Other is myself" (316). Such change is deeply disturbing; indeed, de Beauvoir deems aging more frightening than death since the latter involves a complete transition into nothingness, while the former process promises potentially distressing transformation:

[T]he dead are *nothing*. This nothingness can bring about a metaphysical vertigo, but in a way it is comforting—it raises no problems. "I shall no longer exist." In a disappearance of this kind I retain my identity. Think-

---

7. Mike Featherstone writes of the declining aging body as "misrepresenting and imprisoning the inner self" ("Post-Bodies" 227). Simon Biggs summarizes the arguments of Featherstone and others by concentrating on the "mask motif" to deal with "an antagonism between the ageing body and a youthful 'inner' self" (*Mature* 63). See also Esposito (68–69); Woodward (*Discontents* 60–63).

ing of myself as an old person when I am twenty or forty means thinking of myself as someone else as *another* than myself. Every metamorphosis has something frightening about it. (11, original emphasis)

The experience of self-estrangement is part of the paradox of old age and the overriding sense that "as we age into old age, we are both more ourselves and less ourselves" (Holland 72). This notion of simultaneous gain and loss relies on divisions between internal and external selves that aging into old age appears to augment. In old age tensions between bodily and "true" selves are understood to increase to the point of fracture, giving rise to what Kathleen Woodward has identified as the "mirror stage of old age," which is "the inverse of the mirror stage of infancy. What is whole is felt to reside *within,* not *without,* the subject. The image in the mirror is understood as uncannily prefiguring the disintegration and nursling dependence of advanced age" (*Discontents* 67, original emphasis). To see "one's own aged body with a shock of recognition" (63) is to experience "the *uncanny*" (63, original emphasis). The notion of older persons as inevitably split subjects appears often in writing on aging, both scholarly and fictional. The persistent attention paid to internal, essential, or true selves in aging studies says much about the belief in youth-based identities, and singular, "modern" selves. This insistence on "core" youthful selves betrays the dread of change that provokes aging subjects to reject an altered self rather than admit to transformative identity.[8]

THE UNCANNY

As Nicolas Royle confirms, the uncanny "has to do with a sense of ourselves as double, split, at odds with ourselves" (6). In Freud's influential essay on the subject, the space of the uncanny is marked by the collapse of boundaries, by the strange trespassing into the regions of the familiar, and

8. Such essential selves take a variety of guises in aging studies. Mike Hepworth and Simon Biggs employ the diction of "core selves," which Hepworth describes as a "sense of continuous personal identity. The division of the self into the two dimensions, private and public, acknowledges the existence of individual self-consciousness or a personal sense of a stable and continuous identity" (29). Sharon Kaufman describes identity consistency in terms of "themes," what she terms the "building blocks of identity. Identity in old age—the ageless self—is founded on the present significance of past experience, the current rendering of meaningful symbols and events of a life" (26). Joseph Esposito argues in favor of an "ultimate self," one "that remains the same through aging" (138).

vice versa. The uncanny destabilizes. Royle finds it "impossible to conceive of the uncanny without a sense of ghostliness, a sense of strangeness given to dissolving all assurances about the identity of a self" (16). Here Royle is drawing on the work of Adam Bresnick, who understands uncanniness as a frightening exposure of the instability of selfhood; the uncanny is not "something a given subject experiences, but the experience that momentarily undoes the factitious monological unity of the ego" (qtd. in Royle 16). The uncanny may be provoked by a novel or a film, a painting or photograph, by the everyday (a sound, a smell, an unsettling sight glimpsed through a streetcar window), but its action is internal, which is why "unsettling" is such a suitable description. The uncanny undoes, if only for a moment, one's illusions of peaceful stability, of rootedness. To "unsettle"—"To undo from a fixed position; to unfix, unfasten, loosen" (*OED*)—this is the effect of the uncanny.

Later-life confrontations with temporality, that is, a new or intensified awareness of the differences between past and present selves, often produces uncanny intimations of the fundamental instability of selfhood, as Woodward has indicated. Later life, with its proliferation of personal narratives, can expose the chimerical nature of identity, rendering the subject a contested site, at once familiar and strange, in short, uncanny. My use of the term draws on Freud's famous exploration of the uncanny as "that class of the frightening which leads back to what is known of old and long familiar" (340). In Freud's essay, the uncanny is the chilling resurfacing of buried beliefs, of that which is deeply "known" but repressed.

The uncanny is an experience of doubling, one of ambivalence and contradiction. It has to do with the shocking, even frightening, upset of expectations. It is an unpleasant uncovering, the return of the repressed. Perhaps one of the most widely cited definitions of the phenomenon is Schelling's, which Freud himself employs as a touchstone for his own investigation. Schelling makes the uncanny an experience of unpleasant revelation of "something which ought to have remained hidden but has come to light" (qtd. in Freud 364), an exposure that Freud locates in the psyche: "the uncanny is in reality nothing new or alien but something which is familiar and old-established in the mind and which has become alienated from it only through the process of repression" (363–64). Here the uncanny as collision appears again, this time transformed into the unpleasant confrontation of the conscious and unconscious. It is not merely the strangeness of an event or experience that generates its uncanniness, but the degree to which it disturbs and dredges up something submerged within the psyche. The uncanny is at once strange and all too familiar. Schelling's remarks paired with Freud's references to the mind evoke the psyche in spatial terms: the unpleasant is partially hidden in the dark recesses of the mind, and the failure of this concealment triggers an unwanted confrontation. There can be danger in these recesses. At its most extreme, the uncanny return of the repressed can be a rediscovery of trauma that violently destabilizes the subject. But as my overview of decline ideology and its critics indicates, the overriding association of aging with loss has been called into question. For some, aging into old age may indeed constitute a debilitation akin to trauma,[9] but I think aging and its interpretation tend to be more ambiguous and even paradoxical. Though uncanny confrontations need not be traumatic, they can still disrupt the subject, causing, at the very least, an unsettling of selfhood that is disquieting.

The German word *unheimlich* itself draws attention to the uncanny as an experience of reversals and negations. Freud makes much of the multiple meanings and etymology of *unheimlich*.[10] *Heimlich*, a word associated with home, a place of comfort and familiarity, a collection of positive, homely associations, is upset by the addition of the prefix *un*, which transforms the word into a term of estrangement. But Freud goes further here to point out the multiplicity within the root *heimlich* itself: "on the one hand it means what is familiar and agreeable, and on the other, what is concealed and kept out of sight" (345). Thus, the ostensibly positive root of *unheimlich* is itself tinged with negative associations, with mystery and secrets. Freud's consideration of terminology gestures toward the inevitable cohabitation of the familiar and strange, canny and uncanny: "*Heimlich* is a word the meaning of which develops in the direction of ambivalence, until it finally coincides with its opposite, *unheimlich*" (Freud 347); each term (and its referent) is forever implicated in the other.[11] In

9. I am reluctant to go so far as to identify aging itself as a form of trauma, as E. Ann Kaplan does: "The trauma of aging consists in being *in time* and unable to get out of it. One irrevocably *must* age; one must deal with the ravages of the aging body; and one must confront the fact that death is inevitable. All of which can be experienced as a trauma, which, though basic to human existence, is paradoxically also 'outside human experience' in that no one returns from death" ("Trauma and Aging" 173). Only because Kaplan reads aging primarily as "the increasing series of losses—of bodily function and appearance, of mental agility, of ideologies and values one grew up with, of friends and family" (173) is her trauma hypothesis tenable.

10. Royle conducts a similar investigation into the English term "uncanny" and its etymological sources. Perhaps one of the most important similarities between "*unheimlich*" and "uncanny" is that both are made by negative prefixes, drawing attention to the uncanny as a process of undoing, negation.

11. Royle's investigation into the English variant shows a similar ambiguity: "in

this way the ambiguity of the term itself functions as a metaphor for the phenomenon of the uncanny. In other words, the uncanny already resides within the canny, by definition and as a personal and cultural phenomenon. The uncanny reveals unsettling strangeness buried within the familiar, the stranger hidden within the self.

The uncanny is tightly bound to temporality; the inability to return to past sites and past selves often comes into conflict with our memories of these pasts. Memories can become ghosts that haunt the present. The uncanny can be understood as the cohabitation of tenses, memories of a familiar past rubbing up against the strange newness of the present. Familiarity depends on the interaction of experience and recollection, a concurrence between one's perception of what was and what is. I experience the uncanny when my expectations, inevitably based on memory, are upset; when the familiar, the recognizable, is infiltrated by the strange, the unrecognizable, that is, when the past and present fail to align properly. Because no one has the option of actually living in the past, memories must always be summoned from the vantage point of the present, initiating unavoidable comparisons between what was and what is. Considered in these terms, it seems inevitable that aging will provoke the uncanny: both arise out of temporality.

Consequently old age provides fertile ground for explorations of the uncanniness of self since the inexorability of time challenges any belief in a consistent and stable self. Despite poststructuralist deconstructions of the subject,[12] one's experiences of oneself typically rest on a perceived

---

its archaic past, 'canny' has already meant its opposite ('uncanny'). . . . The similarities between English (or Scottish English) and German, regarding the ways in which 'uncanny' (*unheimlich*) haunts and is haunted by what is 'canny' (*heimlich*), are themselves perhaps uncanny" (11). In Royle's text uncanniness seems highly contagious, if not ubiquitous, already lurking within the most seemingly benign experience. Much of Royle's analysis reveals how the discourse of the uncanny (the term itself, its theorization by Freud and others) is itself uncanny. Indeed, many critics have pointed out the uncanniness of Freud's own essay and its analysis, the ways in which his observations and interpretation appear strategically blind, yet oblivious to their own oversights. Such critics attempt to "articulate what is conspicuously not said in Freud's symptomatic essay or in those of subsequent commentators on the uncanny" (Lloyd Smith 3). Cixous claims that, in Freud's analysis, "Everything takes place as if the *Unheimliche* went back to Freud himself in a vicious interchange between pursued and pursuer; as if one of Freud's repressions acted as the motor re-presenting at each moment the analysis of the repression which Freud was analyzing: the *Unheimliche* is at the root of Freud's analysis" (526). See also Royle 7–8.

12. The study of human identity in the relational terms proposed by semiotics resulted in the idea of persons as entirely determined by language, the subject as

"reality of selfhood," giving rise to what John Paul Eakin calls the "face-off between experiential accounts of the 'I,' on the one hand, and deconstructive analyses of the 'I' as illusion on the other" (4). This central conflict between the theoretical (absent) self and the experiential (present) self is brought to the fore in the study of aging and identity. I maintain that in contemporary culture, aging, particularly aging into old age, forces a confrontation between these competing discourses of selfhood. In aging studies the uncanny most often describes the disconcerting newness of the old body and how the subject experiences the body's image as strange, at odds with the familiarity and continuity of the psyche, termed variously the "core self," "ultimate self," "true self," and so on. Confrontations with the image, such as the "mirror stage" identified by Woodward, represent a distinctly uncanny experience, and the ubiquity of mirror scenes in the literature and films of old age attests to the powerful impact of the reflection on selfhood. But I believe there are other occasions for the uncanny that arise out of old age. Connected to the difficult acknowledgment of the other in the mirror as in fact a part of the internally "young" self is the way that older persons can function as uncanny figures for those around them. Behavior, expression, and personality can all be part of the tension between simultaneous recognition and misrecognition in personal encounters with older persons. For example, somebody one has not seen for many years may present a shockingly changed bodily surface, strangely at odds with the familiarity of their gestures and remarks, the idiosyncratic way with a knife and fork, a recognizable giggle, a peculiar use of diction. The visage of another can seem startlingly "new" as a result of old age, yet at the same time, the younger, more familiar face can be glimpsed at certain moments. A good example of this unsettling strangeness is produced when aged film stars are trotted out at awards shows for recognition of lifetime achievement. The filmic images that precede the entrance of the actor are set into sharp relief by the aged body that enters the stage.

These encounters with the uncanny involving the aged image are common and easily recognizable. But old age can also produce another opportunity for the uncanny that goes beyond the disjunction between an altered image and a perceived "inner" consistency. Indeed, the body, despite its alteration, can provide the only opportunity for recognition after the onset of dementia, a condition that most frequently affects older persons. The

---

"empty outside the enunciation which defines it" (Barthes, *Image* 145). For informative overviews of these developments, see introductory chapters in Butte, Eakin (*Making Selves*), Schwab, and Paul Smith.

radical disruption of memory caused by dementia can make the body one of the only remaining sources of familiarity for others. Changes and deterioration of memory result in the fragmentation or even severance of the person's life narrative, and by implication, his or her identity. For the victim of dementia, even specular recognition is often not possible, and self-estrangement can become painfully severe. Because of the dissolution of language and narrative abilities, the subjective experience of dementia remains largely a mystery. Fiction can attempt to express dementia-afflicted subjectivity, though the difficulties of representing a subject estranged from language and memory tend to restrict such efforts.[13]

The centrality of narrative-based ontologies, such as those put forward by Paul Ricoeur and others (discussed below), means that the disruption and erasure of memory are largely interpreted as an upset and disappearance of selfhood, evoking once again the central paradox of old age as an uncanny site of simultaneous presence and absence. In *Strangers to Ourselves*, Julia Kristeva suggests that subjects always contain the other, that xenophobia is actually a symptom of the rejection of the foreigner within. According to Kristeva, in "The Uncanny" Freud introduces the concept of the fractured self so integral to psychoanalysis and its application: "The uncanny would thus be the royal way (but in the sense of the court, not of the king) by means of which Freud introduced the fascinated rejection of the other at the heart of that 'our self,' so poised and dense, which precisely no longer exists ever since Freud and shows itself to be a strange land of borders and othernesses ceaselessly constructed and deconstructed" (191). The uncanny is unavoidably entangled with conceptions of identity; it exposes cracks in the facade of that essential self that many theorists of aging continue to erect as a shelter from the unsettling changes of age. As Richard Kearney points out, "Kristeva makes the intriguing point that the ultimate stranger of strangers is the shadow of our own finitude" (*Strangers* 76). Old age functions as a manifestation of this frightening shadow, introducing subjects to their own strangeness.

Incorporating Kristeva's argument, with its emphasis on the unavoidability of otherness within, allows one to assert that the discovery of the self's strangeness is the result not of a new condition, but rather of a new

---

13. For example, Mordecai Richler's *Barney's Version,* discussed in chapter 2, switches narrators once the title character's dementia becomes severe enough to seriously inhibit clear communication. More commonly sufferers of dementia are characters observed *by* the narrator, rather than actively focalizing the story; see, for example, Alice Munro's "The Bear Came Over the Mountain" (*Hateship*) and "Spelling" (*Who Do you Think*).

awareness of human difference. Entitling her chapter on Freud "Might Not Universality Be . . . Our Own Foreignness?" Kristeva suggests that because we are all foreigners, "there are no foreigners" (*Strangers to Ourselves* 192), a pattern of logic that can be understood as a comment on otherness in general, exposing the subject's fundamental closeness to that which he or she rejects.

The older subject, as I have argued, is disavowed, at once denied and acknowledged. Old age makes us *aware* of the other within, of identity as always different, multiple, shifting, and contradictory; it shows us how, as Royle puts it, "difference operates at the heart of identity, how the strange and even unthinkable is a necessary condition of what is conventional, familiar and taken-for-granted" (24). Old age is an experience of, or more often a confrontation with, the uncanniness that is always within us; old age simply represents a new awareness of pre-existing strangeness, of the "foreign body within oneself" (Royle 2).

NARRATIVE AND AGING

This foreignness within is part of the nonfixity that results from what Paul Ricoeur identifies as "the temporal character of human experience" (*Time* 1: 3). Subjects experience this temporality in their own aging and in the explanatory narratives they create. Narrative allows subjects to explain, to create meaning in every area of existence, with works of literature and film forming only one small subset of narrative practice. I am particularly interested in the explanatory power of narrative, and in models that stress causality. Ricoeur is emphatic in his association of narrative and explanation: "A list of facts without any ties between them is not a narrative. . . . To explain why something happened and to explain what happened coincide. A narrative that fails to explain is less than a narrative. A narrative that does explain is a pure, plain narrative" (*Time* 1: 148). Ricoeur's emphasis on the explanatory imperative of narrative points to its ontological power, to narrative as a process of making worlds and making meaning. One creates or recognizes a narrative by identifying, elucidating, and even creating relationships between various incidents and characters. According to Ricoeur, this is how human subjects simultaneously create and receive time. Narrative and time are part of a hermeneutic circle: "time becomes human time to the extent that it is organized after the manner of narrative; narrative, in turn, is meaningful to the extent that it portrays the features of temporal experience" (*Time* 3: 3). The constitutive circularity of narrative and time means that any study of aging must inevitably consider questions of narrative. Indeed, if aging can be regarded as a manifestation of human time, narrative and aging are intrinsically, if not constitutively, bound.

Narrative is also tightly bound to questions of identity since subjects' ideas of themselves and others, of their "meanings" as persons, largely stem from their interpretation of their own and others' narratives. It is through the narrative use of language that one comes to understand the self. Anthony Kerby proposes a "model of the human subject that takes acts of *self-narration* not only as descriptive of the self but, more importantly, as *fundamental to the emergence and reality of that subject*" (4, original emphasis). In Kerby's view, "the self is not some precultural or presymbolic entity that we seek simply to capture in language. In other words, I am, for myself, only insofar as I express myself" (41). Some theorists of identity, such as Eakin, remain skeptical of the simple equating of narrative and identity, arguing that a story cannot stand in for "all that we believe we are" (*Making Selves* 102), asserting the importance of other factors, particularly embodiment, in the subject's experience of him- or herself.[14] However, a broad understanding of "narrative identity" can make room for a variety of "selves," even "selves" in conflict. Because narrative is constantly proliferating, one can find a great number of versions of self that might assuage Eakin's fears of exclusion.

The assumption that narrative produces meaning underlies many of the models of aging and late-life identity constructed and employed by aging studies critics. Indeed, the burgeoning field of narrative therapy, discussed in some detail in chapter 2, attests to the potential restorative power of narrative. The preservation of personal narratives is often a defensive strategy that can temper the discomfiting changes of age. But this ontological function of narrative leads us to the problem of the nonnarrativized life: without a story the life is without explanation, without meaning, and by implication the nonnarrativized person is without selfhood. The inescapable emphasis placed on narrative in the production of meaning and identity presents serious difficulties for the victim of dementia or amnesia, whose selfhood is often seen as jeopardized by his or her reduced ability to employ memory in the service of personal narratives. Although those suffering from dementia may still use short-term memories to produce

14. Eakin's own analysis of autobiography and selfhood rests on a pluralistic model of identity based on the work of Ulric Neisser, which regards self-experience as the result of the ecological, interpersonal, extended, private, and conceptual selves (*Making Selves* 22–23).

micronarratives of the immediate past, these narrative fragments are often radically disconnected from one another and fail to contribute to coherent life stories. Memory loss, coupled with the intermingling of actual and imaginary histories, produces a subject disoriented by a disarray of narrative fragments. Dementia presents a most extreme instance of ruptured selfhood. Aging into old age can challenge our conceptions of identity in much subtler ways. Autobiographies, interviews, anecdotes, literature, and film have articulated the numerous ways old age can fray the lines of connection between the various sources of self-identification, exposing change and ephemerality where subjects once experienced an illusion of security and stability.

Narratives of old age in both fiction and film have much to teach us about the mechanics and effects of narrative-based ontologies and their potential straitjacketing of subjectivity. A most extreme example of the anxiety that attends failures in storytelling is the representation in popular culture of the horrified reaction to dementia as a gradual erasure of the self. Consider the saccharine film *The Notebook,* in which Duke (James Garner) responds to his wife Allie's (Gena Rowlands) Alzheimer's-induced failure of memory with narrative. From his notebook, he reads her the story of their life together, using this metanarrative of her life to wrest her true, core self, the one based on narrative memory, from the fog of dementia that has her in its grip. Notably, the narrative he tells is one of heteronormative romance, locating her identity in her choice to devote herself to one man (that would be Duke) over another. Dementia has severed her from her maternal and spousal roles, and her return to them, even temporarily, through narrative is coded as a triumph; during the film's climactic scene in which Allie achieves a momentary lucidity, she clings to Duke and insists he "tell the children I love them." In this film, narrative functions as palliative care, easing Allie out of the disturbing emptiness of nonnarrative living so that she can die peacefully, with narrative coherence, devoted husband at her side.

Experiences of dementia, largely occurring in late life, raise many questions regarding identity and subjectivity, depicting in the starkest terms a subject made strange to him- or herself. How does one interpret the relationship between the disappearance of narrative and the disappearance of the cogent aging subject? If narrative disappears, what, if anything, remains? Are alternative operations of narrative and identity possible, new interpretations of narrative fragments (reminiscence) and the larger narratives that construct lives as teleologies? I assert that film and literature can help theorize responses to such questions in their dramatization of the dissolution of personal narratives and the concomitant phenomenon of the merely present self.

POSTMODERN AGING?

Even within a narrative-based ontological framework, identity functions as a process, shifting to accommodate the changes in one's life story. Ricoeur himself stresses this dynamism in his articulations of narrative identity, conceding the importance, indeed the unavoidability, of multiple narratives. Far from arguing for a metanarrative or fixed identity, his model recognizes the mutability that results from temporality, a mutability that still allows for a persistent subject. Ricoeur's concept of the *ipse,* or self-sameness, incorporates change into some kind of consistency: "self-sameness, 'self-constancy,' can escape the dilemma of the Same and the Other to the extent that its identity rests on a temporal structure that conforms to the model of dynamic identity arising from the poetic composition of a narrative text. . . . Unlike the abstract identity of the Same, this narrative identity, constitutive of self-constancy, can include change, mutability, within the cohesion of one lifetime" (*Time* 3: 246). This temporal, narrative identity obviates the need for the terminology of the "core," "ultimate," or "true" self through its incorporation of change into its very definition.[15] Theories of flexible, mediated selves, such as Ricoeur's, assist in my interrogation of the overly neat division of identity and specularity in the theorization of aging and old age. Such concepts of the self-sameness achieved through narrative incorporate constant change and instability into a vision of identity that I believe invokes the uncanny.

More extreme theories of nonfixity have been proposed in the last few decades by a postmodern turn that urges the discarding of antiquated humanistic conceptions of an inner self in favor of a belief in relativism, the proliferation of signs, performativity, and simulacra. According to such

---

15. The fluidity of the *ipse* allows for human agency and integrity since we are both readers and writers of our narratives (*Time* 3: 246). As David Kaplan explains, by incorporating temporality into identity Ricoeur suggests that "otherness is not external to selfhood but internal to and constitutive of it" (93). Temporality means both that one is, in some sense, other than oneself, and that narratives are always in process and multiple. As Kaplan puts it, "[I]t is always possible both to tell another version of what happened and to tell another story of our lives" (10), and thereby create another version of self. This concept of an adaptable, shifting self disrupts simple distinctions between secure interior selves and their mutable exteriors.

perspectives, Ricoeur's *ipse,* or self-sameness, along with all other models of the self, reflects a fantasy of agency that belies the arbitrariness of subjectivity as a site that has "the status of a mere grammatical pronoun" (de Man 18). The dynamism of poststructuralism and postmodernism has seeped into aging studies and gerontological research, with mixed results. Though some critics have proposed postmodern models of aging, these tend to focus on the bodily adjustments made possible by new technologies, the "bodycare techniques for masking the appearance of age" that further complicate the position of the aging subject (Katz, "Imagining" 70).[16] These critics tend to look at the relationship between consumer culture and embodied aging, pointing out the potential, and perils, of the body as "project" (Turner 257): "new modes of disembodiment and re-embodiment" made possible by "developments in information technology" may alleviate some of the pains of old age (Featherstone and Wernick 11), but the new malleability of the body may also increase pressure to "correct" the signs of aging. As Stephen Katz argues, "the postmodern life course engenders a simulated life-span, one that promises to enhance living by stretching middle age into a timelessness" ("Imagining" 70). Often such discussions perpetuate surface/depth dichotomies in an effort to protect the humanity of the aging self, acknowledging how aging results in an increasing "inability of the body to adequately represent the inner self" (Featherstone and Wernick 7). By and large, social gerontologists insist on something essential beneath the ever-shifting masks of the self, something constant and reliable, a kind of core identity that provides the subject with a sense of continuity, a self that persists over time.[17] My project, on the

16. In some models of "postmodern aging," "ageing is considered as a series of progressive betrayals that let an individual down and come between the self and the multiple identities made available through consumerism" (Biggs, *Mature Imagination* 6–7), furthering the idea, common in aging studies, of selves and bodies at odds. For example, in his study of aging and fiction, Mike Hepworth divides the subject into private and public selves, discussing identity as related to, but separate from, corporeality. He regards the self as a "social process with potential for change throughout the entire life course[;] the ageing of the body does not destroy the self though it certainly produces changes in the relationship between body and self" (34).

17. Katz, Featherstone, Biggs, Esposito, Hepworth, Holland, and Kaufman all invoke various images of a persistent self. For example, Joseph Esposito's philosophical study of aging divides the lifespan into two stages: "the emergence of the ultimate self and the maintenance of the ultimate self" (101). Temporality can also be divided to reflect a sturdy core resistant to the changes of age. In their study of the benefits of autobiographical reflection, what they term "restorying," Gary Kenyon and William Randall differentiate between "Outer Time-Aging" and "Inner Time-Aging" (9–20).

other hand, works to construct an alternate version of postmodern aging, putting aside models of core selves in order to interrogate the mutability of subjectivity.

Throughout this project, I explore models of late-life conflicts of identity within the larger framework of irrepressible uncanniness, while maintaining a skepticism toward the possibility of identity consistency. Like Eakin, I postulate the "self" as "less an entity and more as a kind of awareness in process" (*Making Selves* x). I argue that the dynamism and process of identity, the multiplicity that characterizes "selves" and makes the discourse of "subjects" more preferable, eventually come into conflict with the stasis written onto old age. Dynamism and identity are frozen, fixed by a culture that scripts old age into a small number of rigid categories. In this way age functions very much like other categories of difference, such as gender, race, and sexuality: older subjects are largely straitjacketed by their supposed otherness, offered simplistic, restrictive identities overly determined by their bodies. But aging produces an instability that constantly evades identification; it defies categorization and casts doubt on the dualism of self and other. Instead there is simultaneity, familiarity *and* strangeness. One of the central problems with the inner/outer identity binary is that it denies "internal" uncanniness. I argue that the uncanniness of old age is far more than a shocking confrontation with an unfamiliar reflection; aging, particularly aging into old age, opens our eyes to the ubiquity of uncanniness, and most unsettlingly, to the contradiction that is constitutive of selfhood. Just as Freud reveals how "*heimlich*" is already tainted by its opposite, uncanniness is always already within our most familiar self.

We are, according to Kristeva, always already "strangers to ourselves," a foreignness that is, I argue, harder and harder to deny as we age into old age. It is our awareness of our own otherness that Ricoeur would argue can lead us to become moral agents, able to move beyond simple self/other oppositions to an appreciation of "oneself as another." As such, old age may present the potential for heightened ethical awareness. Indeed, as Kristeva asks, "how can we tolerate strangers if we do not know that we are strangers to ourselves?" (269). Perhaps aging into old age can alert us to our own strangeness in new ways, leading us toward new ethical relations. The obliquely intersecting claims of Kristeva's *Strangers to Ourselves* and Ricoeur's *Oneself as Another* inform much of my interpretation of narratives of aging and my central insistence on old age as a new awareness of a pre-existing condition.

Each chapter of *Uncanny Subjects* begins with a fragment from Freud's "The Uncanny," which together serve not merely as building blocks but as catalysts to ignite discussion and debate. The use of moments in Freud's essay to structure this book reflects the continuing centrality of Freud's ideas in critical explorations of uncanniness and of the fruitful unsteadiness of his claims. Observations, images, anecdotes, and conclusions from Freud's essay provide provocative, often contentious forays into issues integral to the study of aging, issues of narrative and life review, illness and selfhood, gender and doubling. If such an organizational strategy grants Freud the first word in theorizing the uncanniness of aging narratives, it certainly does not give him the last.

Chapter 1 tackles the relation between identity and narrative by focusing on the project of late-life review. In fictional life review narratives, such as Margaret Laurence's *The Stone Angel,* John Banville's *Shroud,* Carol Shields's *The Stone Diaries,* and Cynthia Scott's film *The Company of Strangers,* characters look back at their lives with varying results. In these texts, the project of looking back exposes the mutability of identity, and the difficulty of plotting a life as a single, coherent narrative. These literary and film narratives both employ and rework the "life review" genre, exposing the implications of temporality for self-understanding as characters confront their own uncanniness.

Chapter 2 refines the concerns of the first chapter by attending to narratives of dementia and caregiving in later life, exploring the problem of identity once narrative abilities are disrupted, or even destroyed. In fiction by Mordecai Richler, Alice Munro, and Jonathan Franzen, along with the film *Iris* directed by Richard Eyre, dementia becomes a frightening exaggeration of uncanny identity. In these texts, the interaction between afflicted older persons and their caregivers tests the limits of witnessing and testimonial, provoking the pivotal question: how does one ethically listen to a sufferer who can no longer testify? In this chapter, I argue that dementia entails a distressing, alienating glimpse of the otherness of the other, a vision that can have serious repercussions for the witness.

Chapter 3 turns to the fraught relationship between the aging image and subjectivity in old age, examining photographic and cinematic doubles that appear within various narratives of old age. In stories by Alice Munro and P. K. Page, and the films *Requiem for a Dream,* directed by Daniel Aronofsky, and *Opening Night,* directed by John Cassavetes, visions of doubles result in a blurring of recognition and misrecognition that challenges the subject's sense of self. In particular, *Opening Night* dramatizes the violent clash of young and old selves, following in the tradition of films such as *Sunset Boulevard, All About Eve,* and *Whatever Happened to Baby Jane,* and exposes the damage enacted by age on the specular subject par excellence, the female movie star. These films make explicit the structuring force of gender in old age that is implied in the stories and novels I discuss.

A number of questions propel my investigation into theories of aging, questions that narrative fiction can help us to explore. Some transformations inherent to aging are impossible to deny, but how one interprets these changes, both in oneself and in others, has much to do with how one recognizes and comprehends the subject and subjectivity. How does one understand, adapt to, interpret, live with the seeming simultaneous sameness and difference that accompanies old age? I believe aging can help us, or sometimes force us, to recognize our occupation of a space between singular selfhood and entirely *subjected* subjectivity. Aging into old age can usher us into an uncanny awareness of our own indistinction, our constantly fluctuating status, our own difference. The uncanniness of aging into old age can teach us that the self is always other than it was, other, even, than it is.

CHAPTER ONE

BACKWARD GLANCES
Narrative Identity and Late-life Review

Thus heimlich *is a word the meaning of which develops in the direction of ambivalence, until it finally coincides with its opposite,* unheimlich.
—Freud, "The Uncanny" 347

To be a person is to have a story. More than that, it is to be a story.
—Kenyon and Randall 1

THE NOTION that human subjects are constituted by narrative has become something of a theoretical truism. As Kathleen Woodward puts it, "To *have* a life means to possess its narrative" (*Discontents* 83, original emphasis). The belief in narrative as what Frederic Jameson calls "the central function or *instance* of the human mind" is pervasive and persistent within both popular and academic discourses of identity (13, original emphasis). Still, there are detractors wary of the all-encompassing claims of the narrative identity thesis. For example, in an editorial for the journal *Narrative*, James Phelan considers the risks of what he calls "narrative imperialism," that is, "the impulse by students of narrative to claim more and more territory" (206). More specifically, Phelan is uneasy with the constriction of identity that is the consequence of relying on a single story of self: "I cannot shake the awareness that whatever narrative I construct is only one of many possible narratives and that the relations among the subsets of these possibilities range from entirely compatible and mutually illuminating to entirely incompatible and mutually contradictory" (209).

In this chapter I propose that identity need not be mononarratological; in fact, I argue that aging forces a confrontation with the multiplicity that Phelan posits as undermining narrative identity, a multiplicity I interpret as intrinsic to both temporal identity *and* narrative. This assertion draws on Paul Ricoeur's vision of narrative and time as inextricably connected, the two forming, in his terms, a hermeneutic circle in which "time becomes human time to the extent that it is organized after the manner of narrative; narrative, in turn, is meaningful to the extent that it portrays the features of temporal experience" (*Time* 3: 3). In other words, human temporality makes self-understanding the result of narrative, a causal relationship that becomes increasingly obvious as subjects age.

Philosophers such as Richard Kearney, Alisdair MacIntyre, and Henry Venema follow Ricoeur in asserting that narrative is our primary means of expressing and interpreting a life. As Kearney explains, "[e]very human existence is a life in search of a narrative . . . because each human life is *always already* an implicit story" (*Stories* 129, original emphasis). His philosophical position stresses the innateness of narrative identity, describing every human being as full of "lots of little narratives trying to get out" (*Stories* 130). Henry Venema concurs, claiming that narrative identity provides "a poetic resolution to the problems of the dialectic of narrative and temporal experience" (97). Our temporality is our fragility, and it is this knowledge of the limited nature of life that not only makes our lives into narratives but also compels us to tell our stories: "The limit experience of death is the most sure sign of our finitude. Moreover, it is precisely *because* we are beings who know that we will die that we keep on telling stories, struggling to represent something of the unrepresentable, to hazard interpretations of the puzzles and aporias that surround us" (Kearney, *Strangers* 231, original emphasis). In other words, echoing Ricoeur's hermeneutic circle of narrative and time, human temporality is responsible both for life's incomprehensibility and for our need to attempt to explain it.

As a result, old age provokes a confrontation with the mutability of identities based on the range of accumulated narratives. This confrontation with change and newness often becomes a source of uncanniness as the proliferation of personal narratives exposes the chimerical nature of identity, rendering the subject a contested uncanny site, at once familiar and strange. The space of the uncanny, according to Freud, is marked by the collapse of boundaries, of the strange trespassing into regions of the familiar and vice versa. Aging involves perpetual transformation that unsettles any claims to secure identity, allowing strange newness to intrude into a subject's vision of a familiar self, and undermining efforts to construct coherent life reviews.

In this chapter, I explore narrative-based identity theories alongside several narrative texts that depict late-life review in action: Margaret Laurence's novel *The Stone Angel*, John Banville's novel *Shroud*, Carol Shields's novel *The Stone Diaries*, and the film *The Company of Strangers*, directed by Cynthia Scott. These literary and film narratives both work with and rework the "life review" genre, exposing the implications of temporality for self-understanding.

NARRATIVE IDENTITIES, "HEALTHY" IDENTITIES

The associations between later life and the evaluative backward glance are well established in both popular and academic culture, which often regard life as teleological, moving toward the telos of death, and the subject in old age as a collection of memories, a series of events that constitute the life narrative. Indeed, according to this perspective, human beings inevitably move along a recognizable trajectory: we are born, we grow, we mature, we die. For medical ethicists such as John Hardwig, the biological "facts" are clear: "We are mortal beings, and death is not only the end result of life, but its telos—the aim or purpose for which we are headed biologically" (Hardwig qtd. in Overall 32). Within this linear program, once one enters the realm of late life, there is little of the route left to look forward to, and as a result the gaze is typically directed backward, initiating a re-examination of the past. This is the vision of old age promoted by developmental psychologist Erik Erikson, whose Life Cycle model sees a person aging through eight stages, each of which involves a central conflict between harmonious and disruptive elements (what he terms the syntonic and dystonic), a conflict that must be resolved in order for one to progress to the next stage of life.[1] The final stage, Old Age, involves a conflict between integrity and despair. Integration entails, in Erikson's terms, "a sense of *coherence* and *wholeness*" (65, original emphasis). This sense is

1. Erikson's eight stages—their central conflicts and ideal resolutions—are as follows:

Stage one: Infancy. Basic trust versus mistrust resolving in hope.
Stage two: Early childhood. Autonomy versus shame resolving in will.
Stage three: Play age. Initiative versus guilt resolving in purpose.
Stage four: School age. Industry versus inferiority resolving in competence.
Stage five: Adolescence. Identity versus identity confusion resolving in fidelity.
Stage six: Young adulthood. Intimacy versus isolation resolving in love.
Stage seven: Adulthood. Generativity versus stagnation resolving in care.
Stage eight: Old age. Integrity versus despair, disgust resolving in wisdom.

associated with interpretive recollection since, Erikson asserts, "[looking] back over a long past . . . helps us understand our lives and the world we live in" (6).

Close proximity to "the end," real or imagined, often intensifies narrative impulses, resulting in a process of "life review" that involves close examination of life narratives. As psychoanalyst Henry Krystal explains, "In old age, as in treatment, we come to the point where our past lies unfolded before us, and the question is, What should be done with it?" (78). He implies that one's past must be manipulated to be worthwhile. Though there may indeed be something inherently narrative about human existence, it is only via reflection and expression that such narrativity can be understood. This emphasis on the function of reflecting, of interpreting, produces the subject as an agent, one actively determining the meaning of his or her life, and implies a two-stage selfhood: simply "being" is not full existence; a complete subject ruminates and interprets. For Porter Abbott, survival depends on our ability "to read as well as to write our lives, perhaps in equal measure" ("Future" 539). Narrative identity results from *re*telling by linking events in a causal chain.

The centrality of narrative to selfhood is fundamental to the burgeoning field of narrative therapy, which insists on the psychological benefits of exploring, and often revising, the stories that make up a patient's life. "Restorying" grants the subject a high degree of agency in identity formation involving "a set of stories we tell ourselves about our past, present and future. However, these stories are far from fixed, direct accounts of what happens in our lives, but products of the inveterate fictionalizing of our memory and imagination. That is, we 'story' our lives. Moreover, we *re*-story them too. In fact, restorying goes on continually within us" (Kenyon and Randall 2). The practice of "restorying" is essential to what Gary Kenyon and William Randall term their *"therapoetic"* perspective, which regards life narrative analysis and manipulation as the means to personal *"healing"* (1–2, original emphasis). Restorying "is a therapy for the sane. In it, storytelling (and storylistening) is not merely a method for solving particular problems that crop up in our lives, but has an importance and integrity all its own, as a means to personal wholeness. In this sense, it is a spiritual activity. Through it, *we become more of who we are"* (Kenyon and Randall 2, emphasis added). Even in an ostensibly flexible model of identity maintenance such as restorying, the fantasy remains of a solid, unyielding core, some self prior to narrative that is able to express itself *through* narrative, unsettling the notion of an entirely narrative-based subject. The rhetoric of "becoming oneself" and the diction of "wholeness" and "healing" stress the corrective power of narrative manipulation; narrative therapy assumes some narratives are better, or at least healthier, than others.

A belief in the efficacy of "storying" one's life provides the therapeutic basis for the practice of life review. Life review has a "multifaceted role: to aid the narrator in achieving new insight and peace of mind; to bring closure to troubling events through viewing them from a different perspective; and to restore as far as possible neglected skills or abilities" (Garland and Garland 4). A seminal article on life review by Robert Butler appearing in the journal *Psychiatry* in 1963 was largely responsible for sparking the interest in the topic that continues today. And though the current understanding of the practice may not employ Butler's universalizing rhetoric—he describes life review as a "naturally occurring, universal mental process" (66)—an emphasis on the soothing power of analysis and understanding remains. In their practitioners' guide to life review, Jeff and Christine Garland assert that "[r]eview gives direction to people's lives as they move towards a valued endpoint, along a well-trodden track marked by success stories—and failures" (35). Life review falls within the category of narrative therapy, allowing subjects to optimize their life story through recognition, revision, and even disposal.[2]

But, as my analysis will demonstrate, there are other ways of retrieving and interpreting life narratives and their constitutive memories. For example, Kathleen Woodward takes issue with life review theory, in particular with Robert Butler's version of the practice, which she regards as limiting in its emphasis on the location, or creation, of consistent and coherent life narratives ("Telling Stories" 150). Woodward argues that Butler's life review insists on summary and analysis, on rational order. Instead of life review, she prefers the more open-ended process of "reminiscence," which "does not promise the totality of the life review. It is more fragmentary and partial. Reminiscence is concerned with a certain moment, or moments, in the past" (151). She regards reminiscence as "generative and restorative," less analytical and restrictive than life review (151). In these terms, reminiscence makes room for multiplicity and mutability, the flux of narrative identity promoted by Ricoeur and Kearney. Life review tends to be a process of analytical revision, much like the practice of narrative therapy, attempting to locate *the* life narrative that will provide the aging

---

2. Life review often has "three stages: focusing on what has been learned about self in relation to others; considering whether this learning is still relevant; and recognising what should be retained, revising what is unclear, and discarding what is no longer required" (Garland and Garland 3).

subject with a stable, comprehensible self. Like aging studies theorists such as Kaufman, Esposito, and Holland, psychologists Butler and Erikson assume a singularity of identity, a constancy through *the* life cycle that facilitates comfortable narrative summation in old age. However, as literary and film narratives can make clear in their fabricated "life reviews,"[3] such a process of coherent, enlightening summing up is difficult, if not impossible. *The Stone Angel, Shroud, The Stone Diaries,* and *The Company of Strangers* suggest the problems, and even risks, that result from regarding life as a singular teleology readily available for narrative transposition. These novels and this film suggest that life narratives are multiple and complex, rife with ambiguities and contradictions, with interpretive blindspots, frustrating ellipses. As the various narrators and characters of these texts make clear, "looking back" rarely, if ever, yields a clear narrative of self. Instead, the reading and writing of lives in these texts exposes the very mutability at the heart of narrative itself, wedded as it is to ever-changing temporality.

The therapeutic preference for certain narratives as more appropriate for psychological healing is, of course, part of the legacy of the psychoanalytic "talking cure," which "meets psychological pain with narrative" (Hemmings 109). In psychoanalysis, narrative can become an anodyne as "healthy" stories are made to replace dysfunctional ones.[4] Ricoeur refers to psychoanalytic practice as a corrective foray into a patient's narrative identity, in which the

> process of the cure . . . is to substitute for the bits and pieces of stories that are unintelligible as well as unbearable, a coherent and acceptable story, in which the analysand can recognize his or her self-constancy. In this regard, psychoanalysis constitutes a particularly instructive laboratory for a properly philosophical inquiry into the notion of a narrative identity. In it, we can see how the story of a life comes to be constituted through a series of rectifications applied to previous narratives. (*Time* 3: 247)

3. A number of critics have attempted to categorize fiction "focused on the last phase of life, the stage which prepares for death" as the generic counterpart to the *Bildungsroman* (Fortunati 158). Termed variously *Reifungsroman* (Waxman), *Altersroman* (Westervelt), and *Vollendungsroman* (Rooke), the designated narratives deal with ripening, review, completion. In narratives of this genre, "the aged person no longer occupies a marginal position, but becomes a central character with a complex psyche, around which the interests of the narrative are centered" (Fortunati 158).

4. For more on the narrative implications of psychoanalysis, see Steven Marcus's "Freud and Dora: Story, History, Case History," and Donald Spence's *Narrative Truth and Historical Truth: Meaning and Interpretation in Psychoanalysis.*

Though Ricoeur's elaborations of narrative identity are essential for my own consideration of aging, I diverge from Ricoeur in these questions of narrative rectification. I do not deny that particular narratives may be less painful and more inspiring than others, but I am wary of the assumption that the analysand can be helped to easily substitute and revise bits of stories in order to produce a more comfortable narrative. Rather, I am interested, like Woodward, in narrative identity in its "bits and pieces" and occasional incoherence. If aging is in part an *accumulation* (of memory, of stories), then the older subject is likely a site of conflicting versions, narrative fragments, even "unacceptable" stories. In other words, older subjects, with their large volume of versions, may be particularly susceptible to narrative instability.

Though narrative is able to provide the comfort of meaning and identity, its temporal nature means that it is always fluid, open to revision and retelling. Interpreting the subject as reader and writer of his or her own life means that alternate interpretations and tellings are always available. As Ricoeur himself explains, psychoanalytic rectification notwithstanding, narrative is "not a stable and seamless identity," making it "the name of the problem at least as much as it is that of a solution" (*Time* 3: 248, 249); narrative identity is always in flux as it "continues to make and unmake itself" (249). Though mutability is an unavoidable effect of temporality, narrative subjects often long for the "stable and seamless identity" of totalizing stories, for metanarratives able to encapsulate a life. Ricoeur charts a space of subject-formation between absolute flux and rigid singularity with the notion of the *ipse,* or self-sameness. As discussed in the introduction, self-sameness incorporates the dynamism that results from temporal human existence by locating identity in narrative: "the story of a life continues to be refigured by all the truthful or fictive stories a subject tells about himself or herself. This refiguration makes this life itself a cloth woven of stories told" (Ricoeur, *Time* 3: 246). The productive incorporation of change and cohesion relies on *recognition,* on the subjects' ability to read and write their lives, to "recognize themselves in the stories they tell about themselves" (*Time* 3: 247). Aging, understood as the human experience of time, draws attention to the dynamism of identity that Ricoeur promotes. But despite the ubiquity of narrative-based concepts of identity that would seem to incorporate mutability, change can function as a frightful specter that threatens to upset the illusion of an established and impermeable self. The prospect of multiple versions, multiple selves introduced by aging can provoke a disorienting unsteadiness as distinctions and categories blur, as oppositions refuse to hold, as identity "develops in the direction of ambivalence, until it finally coincides with its opposite"—that is, as identity moves toward uncanniness.

DYNAMISM AND ITS DISCONTENTS

Models of dynamic narrative identity are not without their critics. Many identity theorists, particularly those involved in the study of aging, are uneasy with mutable models of multiple identity, fearful of the relativism and "inauthenticity" that can result from discarding singular selves with verifiable histories. Aging studies critics continue to grapple with the "paradox" of aging, a double movement involving simultaneous gain and loss. Aging's uncanniness, its "paradoxical development in which we are both more and less than we were before" (Schwartz 7), contributes to theories of core identity, obscured, but not essentially altered, by the changes of age. According to such models, the "kernel sentence" (Schwartz 7), the "ultimate self" (Esposito 138), the "core self" (Hepworth 29) remains reliably stolid amid the movement of time. Wariness toward dynamism is often expressed as a deep skepticism toward seemingly aimless, consumerist postmodernism. Aging studies critic Simon Biggs asserts that "postmodern theorizing results in trajectory without teleology. It has movement without direction and makes a virtue out of disconnection" (*Mature Imagination* 66). Elsewhere, Biggs is even more vehement in his rejection of mutable narrative identity, likening it to "a sort of Stalinism for the postmodern mind: a denial of the past as an anchor, as a source of embeddedness for authentic identity" ("'Blurring' the Life Course" 218). So unsettling is the idea of "forgetting," or more precisely, inaccurate remembrance, that Biggs goes to metaphorical extremes, casting the rewriting and rereading of personal narratives as totalitarian manipulation.

Anxiety concerning the potential erosion of the subject reflects a larger critical uneasiness stemming from questioning the autonomy and stability of the metaphysical subject—in short, stemming from the philosophical challenges of postmodern theory. When assumptions about the self's wholeness are replaced by the recognition of the constructedness of the subject, there are aging studies critics who read this as the disintegration of individuality. The "dissolution of the subject . . . [,] its dispersal into a multiplicity of voices" (Schwab 18), is countered by those who insist on some persistent degree of human autonomy and reject what they perceive as the utter helplessness of the entirely "subjected" and theoretical postmodern subject. But postmodern subjectivity is not merely the murky indeterminacy ascribed to it by its critics. A postmodern perspective provides the potential for an open-ended version of identity, one in which the subject is a shifting site inscribed by various discourses. The discursive subject is one prone to revision, one "in process" rather than fixed, part of history rather than outside of it (Hutcheon 37). There is freedom in such multiplicity. Postmodernism makes room for protean, decentered, even contradictory subjects, tolerating doubleness and uncertainty without insisting on wholeness and final resolution (Hutcheon 111). And aging has the capacity to contribute positively to postmodern theories of identity.

The conflict between the postmodern, discursive subject and the lived experience of subjectivity is not easily resolved, and such a task is certainly beyond the scope of this book; but following the lead of narrative theorists such as Kearney and Ricoeur, it is possible to find a productive space of inquiry *between* the desire for phenomenological truth and a secure internal self as expressed by Biggs, on the one hand, and the dismissal of selfhood as ideological, semantic illusion on the other. Kearney echoes Ricoeur's reconciliatory narrative model, arguing that the narrative subject allows "the hermeneutic middle way," positing a "post-metaphysical self in our postmodern culture" (*Strangers* 188). Kearney remains "convinced that it is possible to continue to speak meaningfully of a narrative *ipse*— self-sameness—in the framework of a hermeneutic conversation which takes on board the postmodern assaults on the sovereign cogito without dispensing with all notions of selfhood" (188–89). If subjectivity stems from narration, and such a "memoried self" relies on the past for constructing selfhood, aging is what facilitates subjectivity; only with age can subjects accumulate histories, memories, selves. George Butte reiterates the possibility of Kearney's "middle way" in his claim that "the force that finally limits the centrifuge of the shattered cogito of postmodernism . . . is time experienced in bodies and, more specifically, time in the form of intersubjective narrative" (7). With age we become increasingly aware that we are subjects of time—we bear its traces on our bodies, which appear to belong, often uncannily, to both the past and the present.

A belief in multiplicity, in various, even contradictory selves, makes selfhood possible without risking a plunge into the reductive dualism of inner and outer identity, of true cores and social masks. A mediated subject facilitates flux, contradiction, and ambivalence. In the textual analysis that follows I examine three novels and a film that evoke narrative identity in their dramatizations of the "life review" process. In *The Stone Angel, Shroud, The Stone Diaries,* and *The Company of Strangers,* characters self-consciously narrate the self, confronting, to varying degrees, what Husserl calls "the paradox of human subjectivity: being a subject for the world and at the same time being an object in the world" (178). Characters from these texts shift into a space of unsettling uncanniness as they attempt to negotiate a variety of selves, drawing attention to the simultaneous self/other status of the subject, a new awareness that moves them toward a recognition of what Ricoeur would call oneself as another. To look back is to gaze at the uncanniness of self.

THE STONE ANGEL
Fragile Dualism

In many ways, *The Stone Angel* appears in line with the models of life review fostered by Butler and Erikson in its narrator's appeal to recollection as a means toward self-recognition and the summation of a life. Hagar uses memory to chart a chronological past, alternating between reminiscence and present-day action, a dualist pattern that reveals a split subject struggling to negotiate between competing selves: past and present, young and old, authentic and distorted. Laurence depicts Hagar's attempts to construct a metanarrative of self (albeit a self in conflict) that conjures a distinct subject moving through time in an orderly fashion. In her efforts to arrange and divide her narrative, and therefore her self, Hagar attempts to skirt the uncanny instability produced by mortal life. Despite her desire to discover, even enforce, a singular, authentic identity, divergent, even contradictory narratives thwart her efforts, exposing the mutability and multiplicity concomitant with temporal identity.

The Stone Angel depicts a character struggling to reconcile past and present, and offers a binaristic model of selfhood that corresponds to Hagar's persistent frustration and anger at what she perceives as a delinquent old self that distorts her true, young self. Hagar repeatedly endeavors to deny and resist her own temporality, and by implication, her own narrativity, in the very process of narrating her life story. Despite Hagar's explicit rejection of mutability and uncanniness, Laurence encourages readers to recognize Hagar's *ongoing* strangeness within. The novel's persistent irony, which resides in the gap between Hagar's staunch, independent character and the infirm ninety-year-old woman reliant on the care of others, along with its accumulation of symbols, including the sightless stone angel, and numerous helpless animals, produces a kind of counternarrative, one that seems aware of its own blindness, even when its protagonist is not. The tension between implied author and narrating protagonist generates a doubleness within the text itself, one that, much like the uncanny, at once reveals and conceals internal difference.

Hagar's narrative of her past reveals a subject wrestling with the physical desire she cannot acknowledge or reject. In her old age, when corporeal needs and events have become so undeniable, she continues to battle against her carnality, denying her incontinence and tears:

> [T]erribly, I perceive the tears, my own they must be although they have sprung so unbidden I feel they are like the incontinent wetness of the infirm. Trickling, they taunt down my face. They are no tears of mine, in front of her. I dismiss them, blaspheme against them—let them be gone. But I have not spoken and they are still there. (31)[5]

Hagar similarly refuses to acknowledge her hunger and thirst, and it is this inattention to her bodily needs that causes great suffering at Shadow Point; though she brings crackers and cheese on her journey, she forgets to take along any water. Of course this oversight is also part of the novel's allusive project, which aligns Hagar with various literary characters by multiple allusions. Laurence's Hagar is the lonely "ancient mariner" and the biblical Hagar abandoned to the wilderness, both characters who yearn for fresh water. The various allusions in the novel serve to accentuate the parabolic narrative shape, Hagar's descent into a nadir from which she must struggle to ascend, moving toward (arguably limited) redemption. In Hagar's dualistic narrative, past and present are interdependent, running in parallel lines that dip and rise in unison.

As much as Hagar is telling her story, it is telling her. In fact, an examination of her narratives reveals that this latter transaction, Hagar's constitution via narrative, is dominant. "We are subject *to* narrative as well as being subjects *of* narrative," writes Richard Kearney (*On Stories* 153, original emphasis); but in Hagar's case, the emphasis falls more strongly on "*to*" since her recollections determine her identity yet she often refuses to reflect on her own narrative, functioning more as mouthpiece than as determining agent, or interpretive author. To be sure, there are moments in the text when Hagar seems capable of becoming an interpretive agent, but these moments are fleeting and not sustained. Perhaps the most obvious example is her revelation about pride that comes when the clergyman,

---

5. Donna Pennee's interpretation of the incontinent body in *The Stone Angel* falls within the larger discourse of paradox and contradiction surrounding the novel. She argues that multiple incontinences in the novel expose Hagar as both victim and agent (4). For more on *The Stone Angel* and incontinence, see Alice Bell and Sally Chivers.

Mr. Troy, sings to her. In pain and near death, Hagar is moved to epiph-any, momentarily recognizing the debilitating impact of pride, shame, and fear on her life. The revelation appears in terms remarkably reminiscent of Freud's "uncanny": self-knowledge resides in "some far crevice of my heart, some cave too deeply buried, too concealed" (292). But, as always, the instant of interpretation and insight is fleeting, and Hagar returns to the rigid confines of an identity formed long ago, one "unchangeable, unregenerate" (293). There are several such moments of insight and reck-oning, all of which are brief, painfully achieved, or confined within the haze of semiconsciousness, the insight dissolving as the moment passes.

"Now I am rampant with memory" (Laurence 5): this oft-cited remark occurs early in the novel, initiating Hagar's repeated contact with nar-ratives of the past. The phrase suggests an inversion of the recollecting, storytelling subject. In Hagar's figuration, memory is the active agent that overtakes its subject, and as a result the subject takes on its more subservient meaning as one *subjected*. The *Oxford English Dictionary* reminds us that "rampant" refers to things "[u]nchecked, unrestrained, aggressive. . . . Having full sway or unchecked course in the individual or (more commonly) in general society." The term's etymology is linked to wild animals, and one denotation refers to a beast reared on its hind legs.[6] Clearly there is no space here for calm, contemplative reflections; a ram-pant memory is a wild and domineering force that demands release in the narrative: "Now I light one of my cigarettes and stump around my room, remembering furiously, for no reason except that I am caught up in it" (6). This narrative, this remembered past, determines Hagar, a wildness of recollection she still prefers to the boredom in the present, where she is treated as a thing by "the middling ones" (6), as "a cash crop" (6), and "a calf, to be fattened" (35).

In the voicing of her life narrative Hagar undermines the multiplicity and flexibility of mediated identity. She seeks to maintain a stiff narrative line bisected into before and after, which could allow her to pinpoint the constitution of self and its subsequent perversion. For Hagar Shipley, the unfamiliarity of the self in the present is in direct contrast to the "true" self of her youth, Hagar *Currie*. Yet Hagar's maiden name deconstructs her

6. Sally Chivers's analysis of *The Stone Angel* emphasizes the preponderance of animal metaphors and similes in the novel, suggesting that such "bestial and deroga-tory" vehicles are an effect of the collision between memories of youth and the fearful difficulties of old age. She suggests that such figurative language effects a distancing from the present, from old age, since Hagar can reach the present only through deroga-tory and evasive metaphor, producing a "tenor [that] continually shifts and evades readers" (30).

own nostalgic vision of a youthful, whole self. The obsolete term "currie" refers to "[t]he portions of an animal slain in the chase that were given to the hounds . . . [or] any prey thrown to the hounds to be torn in pieces" (*OED*). In other words, "Currie" signifies the ruin of a wild creature, suggesting that even in her youth, the patriarchal destruction of the "wild," "willful" feminine was already underway—"Currie" being the name passed on to Hagar through her father. Her narrative documents the undoing of that supposedly true, "Currie" self that has led to the disavowed "figure" of the present, one that appears "arbitrary and impossible" (38). Hagar repeatedly locates herself in a long past moment "when I first began to remember and to notice myself" (38). This period of authentic selfhood occurred when she was Hagar Currie, teetering between the domination of two patriarchs: her father and her future husband. In this brief moment of (illusory) freedom, Hagar is on the brink of marriage, giddily defying her father's wishes and not yet burdened by the realities of her ill-conceived union to Bram Shipley. Hagar's father refuses to condone the marriage, but Hagar is determined: "'There's not a decent girl in this town would wed without her family's consent,' he said. 'It's not done.' 'It'll be done by me,' I said, drunk with exhilaration at my daring" (49).[7] Hagar imagines wholeness and freedom in the fleeting liminal space of transition, a space of change that she transforms into a static portrait of authenticity.

So fixed is Hagar on a definitive, youthful version of selfhood that her current status is often a shock: "I glance down at myself . . . and see with surprise and unfamiliarity the great swathed hips. My waist was twenty inches" (56). The selective use of possessive pronouns betrays Hagar's disavowal, articulating her aged body as entirely other, an unfamiliar and unpleasant object at odds with the body, the self, she lays claim to: only the youthful body of the past is "my" body. Ironically, in her diligent emplotment of her life, Hagar locates herself in *images,* rejecting the temporality, the transition intrinsic to narrative. As I discuss in chapter 3, the double is a recurrent trope in narratives of aging, particularly of aging women, and though Hagar Currie does not return with the frightening

---

7. Notably, it is during this liminal moment between men that Hagar's father seems to briefly acknowledge her subject status, calling his daughter by her name:

> Then, without warning, he reached out a hand like a lariat, caught my arm, held and bruised it, not even knowing he was doing so.
> "Hagar—" he said. "You'll not go, Hagar."
> The only time he ever called me by my name. To this day I couldn't say if it was a question or a command. I didn't argue with him. There never was any use in that. But I went, when I was good and ready, all the same. (49)

violence of the spectral fan in John Cassavetes' *Opening Night*, the image of youth in *The Stone Angel* is as undeniable and illusory (and at times even as invasive) as such specters. Hagar's narrative works to deny its own temporality through its efforts to impose constancy—Hagar *is* the young, beautiful unruly girl on the brink of marriage in a first experience of self-awareness—and to deny transience—Hagar *is not* the impoverished aged woman in her husband's overcoat selling eggs at Lottie's backdoor. Nor is she the old woman she sees reflected in a restroom mirror: "My hair was gray and straight. . . . The face—a brown and leathery face that *wasn't mine*. Only the eyes were mine, staring as though to pierce the lying glass and get beneath to some *truer image,* infinitely distant" (133, emphasis added). Hagar's observation reinforces the opposition between youth and age, truth and falsity, resulting in a denial that attempts to consign the distorted, delinquent—that is, aged—self to the space of otherness.

Hagar consistently perceives old age as other, separate from the immutable self she desires. Her denial of change results in a wholehearted insistence on her aged self as artificial, even incorrect. Hagar strenuously disavows temporality, unsuccessfully denying her own difference through othering. Her story emphasizes identity dissolution, a movement *away* from her true, imagistic self, a narrative of aberration. From the vital, familiar self of youth—"Hagar with the shining hair, the dark-maned colt off to the training ring" (42)—to the unfamiliar wife and mother with a "face that wasn't mine," to the "arbitrary and impossible" image in the present (38), Hagar's narrative trajectory is one of loss and diminution. Her inability to tolerate a shifting narrative identity, and her insistence on the fixed and absent image of her memory, inhibit her awareness of otherness *within.* Unable to fully accept the plasticity of narrative identity, Hagar remains trapped in the mournful dualism of past wholeness and present disintegration.

Hagar is not alone in her insistence on temporal segregation. As Kathleen Woodward makes clear, age gradations "ultimately and precipitously devolve into a single binary—into youth and age. Age is a subtle continuum, but we organize this continuum into 'polar opposites'" (Woodward, *Discontents* 6). Woodward identifies such evaluative segmentation as the legacy of a psychoanalytic conception of a bodily ego formed in childhood: "The ego takes shape in infancy; the surface of the body is imagined as smooth, that is, as unwrinkled—in short, as *young*. Thus in Freudian discourse the aging body would be a sign of *deformation*" (10). Consequently, youth often becomes, as Patricia Mellencamp asserts, "a lost object rather than a process or a passage. One can imagine an acceleration of this with age, portrayed as a series of losses rather than achievements, gains, or successes for women. An abnormal modeling of ego or self as an object, often of contempt, rather than a subject can be the rageful result" (281). Frustration, contempt, even rage, are obvious in Hagar's narrative; indeed, the novel opens with an epigraph from Dylan Thomas's "Do Not Go Gentle Into That Good Night." But while Thomas is urging a dying father to rage against death, to rise up vibrant and vital, Hagar's rage is directed both outward and inward in a flailing hatred of time and aging. Trapped as Hagar is in a past image, her narrative is one of frustration, of "*deformation*," since it inevitably moves her away from her beloved youth.

Unable to confront her own temporality and acknowledge strangeness *within*, she is similarly unable to empathize with the other older women patients in the hospital where she is taken after her "rescue" from Shadow Point. She is unnerved by what she can only regard as decrepitude, demanding a private room to protect her from the threat of association with these aged others. She does get her wish, but her move to a semiprivate suite comes just as she is beginning to glimpse the humanity of the other patients, an awareness of their position as subjects. The revelation that Hagar has been talking in her sleep, a disclosure she immediately rejects, suggests the existence of multiple versions, of stories that her conscious cannot abide (259). The narrative voiced in sleep is precisely "everything that ought to have remained . . . secret and hidden but has come to light."[8] Hagar projects otherness onto the other patients, whom she regards as old, infirm nuisances, as abjectly corporeal with their "open-mouthed yawns . . . gaseous belches, volcanic wind" (258). However, this projection is undermined by the shocking discovery that she herself is *one of them* when another patient informs Hagar of her uncanny storytelling:

"Well, what kind of night did you have?" she asks. "Kinda disturbed eh?"

8. This particular secret, sleep-talking, both unveils and maintains Hagar's incomprehensibility, an element of strangeness that can never be entirely domesticated: the uncanny unearthing of dark secrets is always only a partial exposure. An element of irreducible otherness must always remain. This is part of the very uncanniness of Freud's "The Uncanny," which demonstrates the necessary limits to explanation since exhaustive explanation would in effect eradicate the very phenomenon it seeks to explore. In other words, the uncanny and Freud's investigation of it extend to the limits of representation since the term by definition relies on a degree of semantic and interpretive uncertainty.

Her voice has that insufferable brightness that I loathe. I'm not in the mood for her cheerfulness. I wish to heaven she'd go away and leave me alone.

"I scarcely slept a wink," I reply. "Who could, in this place, with all the moaning and groaning that goes on? You might as well try to sleep in a railway station."

"You was the one doing most of the talking," she says. "I heard you. You was up twice, and the nurse had to put you back."

I looked at her coldly. "You must be mistaken. I never said a word. I was right here in this bed all night. I certainly never moved a muscle."

"That's what you think," she says. (258–59)

Hagar's sleep-talking exposes her own strangeness, the multiplicity and unfamiliarity of self that distressingly associates her with the others in the hospital ward. Hers is one of the night voices that speak unbidden when "darkness swarms" (273). These night voices are like "remembered frag-ments painted on shadow" (274); they "stir like fretful leaves against a window":

Tom, don't you worry none—
Mother of God, pray for us now and at the hour of—
Mein Gott, erlöse mich—
You mind that time, Tom? I mind it so well—
I am sorry for having offended Thee, because I love—
Erlöse mich von meinen Schmerzen—
Bram! (275)

It is a shock for Hagar to recognize her own cries among the others; indeed, "Some time elapses" before she recognizes her voice (275). Hagar's outburst appears as one fragment within an unattributed list of speech that makes her voice one of many in a chorus of sleep-talking. Hagar's recognition briefly pierces through the protective blindness that makes us "refuse to acknowledge ourselves-as-others" (Kearney, *Strangers* 5). Hagar momentarily glimpses, or more precisely, hears, herself-as-other in her uncanny utterance: she discovers a voice and a story that is her own, that is *her*, and yet is unfamiliar. Aging, and the association with other aging women, move Hagar into a space of uncanny recognition in which the illusion of the singular, authentic self begins to dissolve into multiple ver-sions. As philosopher Henry Venema explains in his inquiry into Ricoeur's theory of narrative identity, "there is no meta-narrative that can totalize my experience. Narrative identity is an identity of various stories" (97). The unbidden voice, speaking in fragments, speaking from sleep, speaking alongside many others, divulges the cacophonic self: unstable, various, at once other and self.

But this uncanny recognition is cut short when Hagar is whisked away to the semiprivate quarters she had requested. In her new room, which she shares with a young woman hospitalized for an appendectomy, Hagar quickly returns to her exclusive identification with the "lost object" of youth: "I was quite slender at your age," she tells the thin, young nurse who ministers to her, "I had black hair, long, halfway down my back. Some people thought me quite pretty. You'd never think so to look at me now" (283). Once again Hagar locates herself in a static memory that makes time into a process of dissolution and paradoxical inflation, since it magnifies the body's importance by "deforming" it. She shares her new room with a young woman whose youthfulness quickly inspires Hagar's empathy, unlike the old women of the public ward, who initially prompted irritation and disgust.[9]

The novel emphasizes a static vision of selfhood that equates time and change primarily with debilitation in its framing image of the stone angel; in her full (though blind) glory at the outset, she is altered by time at the novel's end: "she stood askew and tilted. Her mouth was white. We didn't touch her. We only looked. Someday she'll topple entirely, and no one will bother to set her upright again" (305). Original integrity is set against the collapsed future, the metonymic angel neatly bracketing Hagar's narrative of her own fall.

However, though the novel does employ these stone angel images as a frame, the weather-beaten angel does not close the novel. The novel's actual ending, two pages later, gives temporality the final word. The final lines, like the sleep-talking scene, rupture the neatness of the singular self, the simple bisection of Hagar's life into before and after. Hagar's narrative is aborted by mortality and the novel's concluding fragment, "And then—" (308), achieves a simultaneous suspension and triumph of time. This artificial maintenance of the present—the reader is always here, on the verge, unable to move to the next moment—creates an ending that flouts closure.

9. Despite the fact that her roommate, Sandra Wong, is a young Chinese-Canadian woman, Hagar more easily identifies with her than with her contemporaries in the previous ward. Here we see evidence of Woodward's claim that "in advanced old age, age may assume more importance than any of the other differences which distinguish our bodies from others" (Discontents 16). Hagar easily overlooks ethnicity in order to identify with youth.

As a result, the novel, and by extension, Hagar, can be always *on the verge of* and concluded at once. The uncanniness Hagar refused to accept finds her at her death in this fragment, this simultaneous presence and absence, this unfinished completion.

The Stone Angel depicts a character struggling to reconcile past and present, and presents a binaristic model of self that corresponds to Hagar's persistent frustration and anger at what she perceives as a delinquent old self that distorts her true, young self. Hagar repeatedly endeavors to deny and resist her own uncanniness, an uncanniness that she only glimpses at various points in her narration. Though her own awareness is fleeting, the implied author encourages readers to recognize Hagar's *ongoing* strangeness within. The novel's tone, duplicitous diction, and accumulation of symbols produce a kind of counternarrative, one that seems aware of its own blindness, even when its protagonist is not. The tension between implied author and narrating protagonist generates a doubleness within the text itself, one that, much like the uncanny, at once reveals and conceals internal difference. Many "life review" fictional narratives grapple more overtly with the uncanny nonfixity of identity enforced by human temporality. While Hagar narrates her childhood-to-death story of her life, fictional narratives can reveal characters negotiating a panoply of life stories that problematize the summarizing and analysis involved in life review, raising thorny questions about identity and ethical commitment.

"SHIFT AND SLIDE"
Narrative Multiplicity in *Shroud*

> "*Grown old, the imagination, as I have been finding out, tends to play unnerving tricks. . . . The familiar will shift and slide, will change places with things never seen before. A known face will turn into that of a stranger, a window will open onto a vista, menacing and dark, that was not there a moment ago.*"
>
> —Axel Vander *in* Shroud 223

John Banville's novel *Shroud* is the account of narrator Axel Vander's efforts to set the record straight, to "explain myself, to myself, and to you, my dear" (4). The ghostly interlocutor, "you," is gradually revealed to be Cass Cleave, a young critic who has found evidence that would expose the celebrated philosopher as a perpetrator of identity theft. Cass's material evidence, a newspaper clipping that shows a young "Axel" with the real Axel Vander, a friend of his youth whose identity he eventually assumed, forces the old philosopher to confront the lingering traces of the self he has struggled to shed. Axel imagines his divorce from his own past in a grotesquely visceral image of flaying, picturing his former self as a hideous anchor of empty skin: "I had thought I had shaken off the pelt of my past yet here was evidence that it would not be sloughed, but was dragging along behind me, still attached by a thread or two of dried slime" (7). From the vantage point of a debilitated, uncomfortable old age, Axel becomes newly aware of this and other persistent "pelts," and so his narration becomes an exploration of the many versions of his life, a project that is seemingly at odds with his own antihumanist philosophical legacy,[10] which decries the very notion of identity.[11]

The discomfiting changes of old age coupled with a forced confrontation with an unpleasant trace of a disowned personal history provoke Axel to reexamine the "primordial darkness" of his past with its "scattered . . . points of cold, hard light, immensely distant, each from each, and from me" (1–2). These "scattered," alienated selves continue to burn in the darkness, despite Axel's various efforts to extinguish, or at least deny, them. The novel charts a subject begrudgingly exploring his own selfhood from a wide variety of positions (as narrator and interlocutor, subject and object) that move him further and further into the space of uncanny apprehension. In a sense, Axel Vander is haunted by himself, by the very possibility of selfhood, which he has spent his career decrying as illusion. His effort to explain himself, that is, to tell the stories of his life, or more accurately, lives, devolves into a series of versions, a jumble of voices. Axel's own narration proposes, perhaps inadvertently, the possibility of a middle ground between entirely verifiable or illusory identities,

10. Axel's philosophical theories, along with his hidden past tainted by unsavory Second World War collaboration, are part of the character's connection to deconstructionist Paul de Man, whose numerous essays for a Belgian collaborationist newspaper were discovered posthumously. Much like Axel Vander, de Man's narratives are multiple and contradictory, calling into question any definitive account of the man at once deconstructionist, Sterling Professor at Yale, collaborator, anti-Semite. *Shroud* grapples with the implications of a philosophy of multiple and shifting meaning and how the instability of narrative identity can be manipulated in order to conceal and mislead. But in the cases of both Axel and de Man, the deception eventually falters, and that which "*ought to have remained . . . secret and hidden . . . come[s] to light.*"

11. According to Elke D'hoker, an attention to the difficulty of securing stable selfhood recurs throughout Banville's fiction: "the male voice in Banville's texts is always that of a slightly grotesque, slightly uncanny outsider who contemplates the world and its creatures, others and himself" (1). The uncanny is important in Banville's fiction, but especially so in this fiction of the aging narrator.

replacing Axel's early insistence on revealing his true self, "some small precious thing" (5), with a more dynamic identity able to incorporate change and even duplicity. By moving through various narratives and perspectives, Axel gains some awareness of his own difference and, by implication, an increased ethical understanding and even "the possibility of redemption" (5). Narrative both provides a means of affirming and creating selfhood and offers an opportunity for exploring the instability of that selfhood.

For Axel, "the onset of extreme old age" is experienced as "a gradual process of accumulation, a slow settling as of soft grey stuff, like the dust in the untended house, under which the once sharp edges of my self are blurring" (14). The novel's early chapters explore the uncanniness of this "blurring" that makes the self so eerily strange and familiar. Initially, it is the difficulties of the aged body that are uncanny, and Axel imagines his corporeality, his "suety old flesh" (6), as affliction. He has the uncanny sensation that he is "falling off [him]self" (6), recalling the paradoxical position brought about by aging, one of simultaneous presence and absence. For Axel, old age is an experience of being at once himself and other than himself, an uncanny subject position that gives rise to a paradoxical image of self-alienation: "That is what I am, a dead weight hung about my own neck" (6). But, as we learn over the course of the novel, this identity of difference, this otherness encountered in old age, is merely an exacerbation of an ongoing strangeness within. These vagaries of the flesh alert Axel to a long-lingering unsteadiness of selfhood that he can now no longer deny. Axel's "accumulation" has been lifelong: names, nationalities, stories, and deceptions. Old age is often popularly figured as an accretion of time that goes hand in hand with the amassing of narrative. The image of the "blurred self" powerfully illustrates the unsettling recognition of uncanny identity that old age can lay bare. The high resolution of the illusory unified self, with its familiar, stable body and its identifiable life narrative, can give way to the indistinction of temporal identity, to fluidity, to instability. *Shroud* effectively captures the ambiguity of uncanny old age, demonstrating the ethical potential of the "blurred self" along with its frightful alienating effects.

The novel's opening line, "Who speaks?," underscores its preoccupation with the ethical dimensions of narrative authority. Just as the plot is a gradual revelation of identity appropriation, the narration comes to divulge its own duplicity, revealing a single narrative agent behind a variety of voices. The dual perspectives in the novel, Axel's first-person narration and Cass's third-person focalization, collapse into one another as the reader realizes that Cass's reflections, insights, emotional responses, have all been supplied by Axel himself. Already dead at the start of the novel, Cass is unable to share her perspective, and Axel's version of her is the only one available. Axel does not assume her voice—his is the only first-person narration—but recreates her subjectivity in the details of focalization. Through Cass's constructed perspective Axel consigns himself to the position of aged other, entirely estranged from her. She observes his naked body as a temporal object, a vision of alterity that the reader later learns comes from Axel himself:

> There were brown moles on his back, and long grey hairs sprouting on his shoulder blades, and the loose flesh of his lop-sided rump wobbled when he walked. She had never seen anyone so huge, so naked and so defenceless. She pondered in mild amazement the mystery of time and time's damagings. Soon, in a very few years, a decade at most, surely, he would be gone, and all that he had been and was now would be no more. (121)

Only one page later the novel delivers the details of Axel's duplicity, that he himself is the source of these impassively objectifying observances. The third- and first-person pronouns converge to produce a cubist image of selfhood, one that incorporates a disorienting variety of identity positions. The manipulation of perspective responds to the novel's opening query by exposing the impossibility of the question, which relies on a fantasy of stability and singularity. In these few pages, tellingly positioned at the very centre of the novel, the possibility of essential selves shatters:

> He drew his hand from under the bedclothes and held it up for her to see. "With this I wrote those articles you found," he said. "Not a single cell survives in it from that time. Then whose hand is it?" He, I, I saw again the empty bottle on its side, the mauve pills in my palm. I closed my eyes. I listened to the wind washing over the rooftops. The girl rose and came forward and knelt beside the bed and took my hand in both of hers and brought it to her lips and kissed it. I. (122–23)

Then whose hand is it? Old age is here a revelation of temporality in its starkest terms. The uncanny paradox of the age-altered self moves the subject into the space of alterity and back again as Axel experiences, in quick succession, his body as time-damaged object and active agent, his voice as another's and then his own. Between the "inexistence of the self" that Axel pronounces in his professional life (122) and the "enduring core of selfhood amid the welter of the world" that he longs for (18) is the liminality of uncanny identity, that of the perpetually aging subject existing in time, in narrative.

The uncanny vision afforded by age moves Axel toward an ethical understanding unavailable in his youth. In particular, it is the process of narrativizing his many pasts that leads him toward this new ethical insight. Kearney regards narrative as means for ethical understanding since it facilitates a navigation of the space between self and other, even leading toward "*narrative understanding:* a working-through of loss and fear by means of cathartic imagination and mindful acknowledgement" (*Strangers* 8, original emphasis). Narrative can help us explore the space between self and other, "build[ing] paths between the worlds of *autos* and *heteros,*" paths of understanding that can "help us to discover the other in our self and our self in the other—without abjuring either" (*Strangers* 10). Kearney calls his model, "diacritical hermeneutics," a "third way," one beyond romantic and radical visions of alterity, that promotes the possibility of "intercommunion between distinct but not incomparable selves. . . . Between the *logos* of the One and the anti-*logos* of the Other, falls the *dialogos* of oneself-as-another" (*Strangers* 18). Axel's multiple life narratives show both the liberatory potential and difficulty, even danger, of charting this "third way," a way that opens his eyes to his own otherness and to the humanity of other people. Telling his story, explaining his life, demands the incorporation of alternative perspectives and voices because a single, constitutive story does not exist. Axel's narration involves the recognition of the relativity of identity that makes any story only partial, a fragment of a larger cluster of often conflicting narratives.

Beyond the obvious duality of Axel Vander as both Axel and the young Jewish man who precedes him is a phalanx of selves that unsettle any claim for an authentic identity, a multitude of performances that Axel readily acknowledges: "I am, as is surely apparent by now, a thing made up wholly of poses" (210). Axel's new, age-induced sensitivity to the fluidity of his own selfhood eventually moves him toward the other, enabling novel experiences of empathy and understanding. Axel's poetic imagination moves him *in the direction of ambivalence;* indeed, the closer he becomes to Cass, the more the canny and uncanny seem to trade places, and even to converge. The uncanny vision narrative endows can move one into the space of ethical understanding since "it is exactly this double-take of difference and identity—experiencing oneself as another and the other as oneself—that provokes a reversal of our natural attitude to things and opens us to novel ways of seeing and being" (Kearney, *On Stories* 140).

Axel's experiences with Cass, and his self-alienating assumption of her narrative perspective, put Kearney's ethical claims for narrative into action. But redemption, even its possibility, comes with a price, demonstrated in the novel's final lines. Axel's narrative experiments expose him to the staggering responsibility that comes with insight. Cass's death, along with former lover Kristina Kovac's terminal cancer, produces a painful knowledge of interconnection and responsibility: "The city is quiet at this time of year. The dead, though, have their voice. The air through which I move is murmurous with absences. I shall soon be one of them. Good. Why should I have life and she have none? She. She" (257). Between presence and absence, sound and silence, life and death, Axel hovers in the liminal space of uncanny knowledge. The narrative becomes an overt exchange between self and other as Axel takes responsibility for animating Cass's narrative at his own expense. In *Shroud,* old age prompts a narrative revisitation of the past that provides Axel with an uncanny vision of himself and Cass as simultaneously selves and others.[12]

Certainly self-reflexive life narratives need not be so dire or traumatic. For example, a novel such as *The Stone Diaries* by Carol Shields is able to combine a multivocal point of view with a high degree of playfulness. The story of Daisy Goodwill is told from a narrative voice that shifts between first and third person, producing a twisting narrative in which the first-person narrator often views herself as a distinct character, referring to herself in the third person. The novel includes a variety of voices besides Daisy's, including characters who observe and interpret her, resulting in a multifaceted subject composed of many, often conflicting narratives. In chapters such as "Sorrow," the plethora of narrative voices attempting to explain

12. I recognize that my somewhat optimistic reading of Axel's appropriation of Cass's perspective overlooks Cass herself. There are a number of questions left to consider, particularly: What about Cass? Does she confront her own otherness through her interaction with Axel? Is she merely a rhetorical tool for Axel, a means to his own self-exploration? Axel himself acknowledges his exploitation, how he reached himself *through* her: "I used Cass Cleave as a test of my authentic being. No, no, more than that: I seized on her to be my authenticity itself. That was what I was rooting in her for, not pleasure or youth or the last few crumbs of life's grand feast, nothing so frivolous; she was my last chance to be me" (210). But such a blunt exposure of self-interest shows the glimmer of a new awareness of others and Axel's responsibility to them, if only expressed here in the negative. Since the novel is constructed as the product of a single narrator, the inclusion of sections from Cass's point of view is evidence of Axel's extended contemplation of the subjectivity of the other, indicating a new willingness to move away from the solipsism that has protected him from guilt and responsibility for so long. As indicated in the lines above, at the novel's conclusion, Axel's life appears only in relation to these lost others.

Daisy's depression creates a cubist effect, representing the subject from many perspectives at once, a multiplicity of views that emphasizes the difficulty of determining a single version of selfhood. This commingling of perspectives suggests that identity is a collision of roles, experiences, bodies, memories, opinions; subjects are always shifting and multiple. Writing of herself, Daisy undermines the possibility of true, authentic selves: "She is not always reliable when it comes to the details of her life; much of what she has to say is speculative, exaggerated, wildly unlikely. . . . Daisy Goodwill's perspective is off. Furthermore, she imposes the voice of the future on the events of the past, causing all manner of wavy distortion" (148). Daisy's narration self-reflexively draws attention to the impossibility of a single, true, linear life narrative, exposing the past as malleable, "distorted" by memory and narrative.

The Stone Diaries is an obvious allusion to Laurence's *Stone Angel*: both depict characters using memory to reconstruct their lives from childhood through old age and death. But while Laurence uses a single, definite perspective, to engage in life review, Shields employs multiple narrative perspectives in order to maintain ambiguity, undermining the demands of linear narrative and authentic selfhood. This contrast is most prominent in the title symbols: the stone angel in Laurence's novel is a grave marker that signifies family heritage and the blind pride that is Hagar's downfall. *The Stone Diaries* also contains a stone memorial; however, this creation is unnamed, unfinished, and nonrepresentational. The perpetually growing stone tower that Daisy's father erects after the death of her mother remains ambiguous, potentially meaningless. The widower simply cannot stop building, though the purpose of his labors remains obscure. Eventually the expanding tower becomes a kind of tourist attraction, drawing curious visitors who inevitably ascribe some imaginary meaning to the tower. The narrator relates such interpretations without comment, refusing to confirm or deny the structure's "true" meaning or purpose. Instead, the stone tower remains amorphous and impenetrable, both its physical and symbolic structures ever changing.

In both *Shroud* and *The Stone Diaries* the experience of old age enables a multifaceted look backward, a view that incorporates the protagonist as both subject and object. Near the end of Shields's novel, when the protagonist seems to narrate from beyond the grave, the shape-shifting narrator asks the question so central to life review, namely "What is the story of a life?" (340). The protagonist-narrator, Daisy Flett, tries to maintain a chronological narrative that moves through the trajectory of her life, "[t]o keep the weight of her memories evenly distributed. To hold the chapters of her life in order" (340). Indeed, the novel itself is organized into discrete life stages, with chapters entitled "Birth, 1905," "Childhood, 1916," or "Illness and Decline, 1985." Despite her ongoing efforts to "keep things straight," Daisy is unable to avoid "spurious versions" that complicate the simple narrative trajectory of her life (340, 341). The novel's incorporation of multiple narrative voices and of multiple (fictionalized) historical traces (archival photographs, newspaper clippings) belies the possibility of any "straight," singular narrative. Daisy appears as both subject and object, but it is the onset of old age in particular that provokes the most radical dissolution of boundaries and an uncanny blurring of the self that presents Daisy Flett as a grandmother outside of the narratorial "I," established at the novel's opening as Daisy herself: "Does Grandma Flett actually say this last aloud? She's not sure. She's lost track of what's real and what isn't, and so, at this age, have I" (329). The multiple references to this single person ("Grandma Flett," "she," "I") announce the uncanny vision of old age, the blurring of selves and of stories, of reality and fiction initiated by the dizzying project of life review.

As in *Shroud,* narrative in *The Stone Diaries* at once reveals and upends identity, complicating the narrator's (and perhaps the reader's) desire for a discrete, knowable self. This is part of the uncanniness of aging into old age—the proliferation of stories tangles the narrative thread subjects seek to tease out. Even beyond this proliferation of stories, the uncanny position of the older person can initiate a more extreme recognition as awareness of multiplicity leads to glimpses of one's own alterity. The replacement of autonomous, discrete "life review" with multiple versions can lead one into the often disorienting space between self and other, a glimpse of oneself as another that means the discovery of uncanny identity.

STRANGERS, FAMILIARS
Cynthia Scott's *The Company of Strangers*

So far, my analysis of life review narratives has dealt with novels largely concerned with a particular narrating subject. Though *Shroud* and *The Stone Diaries* employ a number of narrative strategies that facilitate a variable point of view, both novels have easily identifiable protagonists, central characters whose stories, though various and shifting, are the narrative's primary concern. *The Stone Angel* is clearly Hagar Shipley's narrative, just as *Shroud* is Axel Vander's, and *Stone Diaries* is Daisy Flett's. The film *The Company of Strangers* (1990), directed by Cynthia Scott, eschews such a restricted focus, depicting instead a group of self-reflexive older characters chatting, singing, dancing, fishing, eating, gazing, and of course, reminiscing. The film's very loose narrative involves this group of women on a bus tour of Quebec. During a detour from their route to see the country place where a member of the group, Constance, "spent the best years of her childhood," the group becomes stranded in the wilderness. There is little sense of urgency over their situation, and the "company," which includes seven women age sixty-five and older, along with their twenty-seven-year-old bus driver, are variously shown exploring the landscape, admiring the views, playing cards, and watching the birds. The minimal plot, easily summarized—the bus breaks down, the women take refuge in an abandoned house and spend a few days in this pastoral wilderness before being rescued by a seaplane—allows for the inclusion of various narrative fragments, anecdotal discussions of personal histories, reflections on present aches and pains, and scenes of quiet gazing in which solitary characters are afforded time to look and think.

In a sense, my analysis of the film takes its cue from its title, *The Company of Strangers,* which draws attention to the cohabitation of familiar and strange.[13] I argue that the film maintains the paradox of its title, the older women existing as both "strangers" and "company" for the film's audience as well as for one another. The film provides space for many small narratives of the past, of daily existence, of old age, that do not easily fit together in service of a larger plot. As a result, spectators glimpse the multiple locations of identity, coming to know something about each character, without necessarily knowing the character. That is, the fragments available to us create not whole portraits but splintered representations that dispel any fantasies of complete or fixed identity. The women self-consciously reflect on old age and tell stories of their pasts, but these narratives are partnered with the dynamism of life in the present, and the creation of new narratives.

The film's hybrid genre, which blends fiction and fact, scripted and improvised dialogue, contributes to and even facilitates the fluctuating position of each woman as subject/object, aging/aged, familiar/strange. The film's generic instability, the hovering between categories of "authentic" and staged, is just one of many productive instabilities that mark *The*

13. *The Company of Strangers* is the film's Canadian title. In the United States, the film was released under the title *Strangers in Good Company,* a title that, though maintaining the cohabitation of the original Canadian title, loses, I believe, some of the uncanny potential of the former.

Company of Strangers.[14] Made in the tradition of the National Film Board of Canada's Alternative Drama program, the film combines conventions of fictional filmmaking (dramatic contrivance, some scripting) with those of the documentary (a cast of nonactors, the use of actual personal histories and photographs) (Stukator, "Pictures" 239). Angela Stukator identifies this incorporation of typically antithetical generic conventions as one of great political potential, able to "challenge a number of related distinctions," including "story and history, fabrication and 'truth,' performance and being, concealment and appearance" (240). Catherine Russell also analyzes the film's many instabilities, particularly its creation of a "complex spectatorial position, one which is at once fixed and shifting" (213). However, she is critical of such instability: "If the film has an ideal spectator, it is not me, or anyone else who can see through its occasionally awkward staging, its tokenist selection of women, and its shaky narrative premises. . . . Neither an art film, nor a feminist film, *The Company of Strangers* offers a disjunctive, dislocated form of address" (213). I see more positive potential in *Company*'s unstable generic status and its inclusion of multiple, disparate narratives, which challenge narrative totality and identity synthesis.

The hybrid genre, which allows for a very loose narrative structure, facilitates the preservation of difference within the creation of "company." Over the course of the film each of the seven women tells stories about her life, reminiscing about youth, motherhood, love, illness, death, and mourning.[15] These anecdotal narratives provide the various characters with the

14. The more recent, seemingly oxymoronic phenomenon of "reality television" also tests our definitions of truth and reality, but with very different results. In these programs, authenticity is emphasized, as the genre title attests, and the role of staging, scripting, and other forms of crew interference is strenuously denied, whereas *The Company of Strangers* maintains, and even nurtures, an ambiguity of genre and origins.

15. It is the seven older women who are the primary storytellers. We learn nearly nothing about Michelle, the young bus driver. Instead of telling stories, she functions more like an interviewer, asking questions rather than answering them. The exclusion of her narratives is evidence of the film's devotion to the older women; *The Company of Strangers* is a film about women over the age of sixty, and as a result Michelle must remain marginal. Interestingly, even the youngest of the "older" group, Catherine, age sixty-five, remains somewhat peripheral—she tells fewer anecdotes and is given less screen time than the other six. We see her listening to devotional music and attempting to fix the bus; she explains to Michelle that she is "married to God," but we learn little else about her life history. Such inattention enacts a reversal of traditional characterization: the older women are the most developed characters, while the younger women seem almost unknown and more prone to stereotyping.

opportunity to explain themselves, to understand and express themselves as selves in accordance with models of narrative identity. Unlike exhaustive and analytical life review, anecdotes are brief and fragmentary, presenting a particular memory that provides only one aspect of a character's narrative identity. These anecdotes fall into the category of "reminiscence," the manner of recollecting Woodward identifies as "generative and restorative" potential, able to "generate the future for the reminiscing subject and not just to revivify the past" ("Telling Stories" 151, 160). In *The Company of Strangers* a variety of kinds of memorializing occur, resulting in a heterogeneous collection of narratives that also challenge the teleological or evaluative efforts of "life review." Certainly identity arises from narrative in *The Company of Strangers*, but the variety and fragmentation of these narratives facilitate a fluidity of identity that maintains strangeness, gaps, and even otherness.

The identifying narratives in the film occur in conversation, the characters functioning as audiences for one another, surrogates for the film's larger audience of spectators. Mary tells Cissy of the struggles she faced as a lesbian in the entirely heteronormative and largely homophobic society of her youth. Cissy tells Mary of the stroke that left her paralyzed, laid up in the hospital for weeks counting windowpanes. Later, Winnie describes to Alice her monotonous job in a cigarette factory during her youth and Alice responds with an anecdote about her own "sleepy" factory job, wiping bottles before fixing them with a ribbon. Constance talks bitterly of her art studies relinquished for motherhood, her life overtaken by the responsibilities of "mating and breeding." Catherine speaks of her devotion to God. Beth sadly recalls the death of her son, which has overshadowed her life. These are only a sampling of the anecdotal narratives that compose the film, stories that show how "everybody's life is more or less interesting," as Mary claims, because, as Cissy concurs, each one is "a drama."[16] In her analysis of the personal histories Russell claims the "fragments of biography" focus primarily on sacrificial stories, describing the women's narratives as largely determined by "devotion to family, or, in the case of Catherine, to the Church" (215). Russell employs as evidence some of the film's most painful anecdotes: Constance's abandoned studies, Cissy's fear of losing her only son, Beth's loss, Alice's hatred of her first husband (215). By limiting her discussion to narratives of loss, Russell is able to construe Scott's "filmmaking process [as] a mechanism of redemp-

16. Catherine Russell would disagree with such optimism, describing the women's lives as "really rather banal" (213).

tion" (218), stressing the film's activation of pathos in the viewer. But what of the less obviously "sacrificial" narratives, what of the many scenes that affirm presence and activity? I believe it is the tension *between* absence and presence in the film, in the wide variety of narratives presented, that is part of its productive potential.

Alongside the conversational narrative anecdotes, the film includes scenes of nonverbal physicality, quiet moments of looking, as well as scenes of everyday activity, such as dancing, eating, playing cards. The activities in the present suggest that the women's life stories do not have an obvious teleology, but instead, remain very much in process and undetermined. Though the film's loose narrative works toward a climax (the arrival of the seaplane), it lacks clear movement toward this moment; there is no great central conflict or lesson learned. Indeed, as Stukator argues, the prolonged images of the various women quietly gazing and thinking actually serve the "film's project of challenging fixed, stable terms of identity," since such images delay the film's narrative flow and interrupt its dominant style (242). I would take this argument even further: the diegetic[17] silences are an assertion of the present tense, of presence that counters pastness and the loss inherent in recollection. In these quiet moments the characters most powerfully function as others; the familiarity of candid conversations and anecdotes is replaced by silence, their subjectivity rendered opaque.

Though in some sense *The Company of Strangers* portrays old age as a time of reflection and thoughtfulness, an association strengthened by the pastoral setting and the soundtrack of Schubert and Chopin, it does not smooth over the cracks in such a peaceful façade, acknowledging that this Romantic depiction is only a partial portrait. There is much talk of discomfort, hunger, loneliness, pain, fear, and longing, and these tensions, along with the incorporation of multiple contradictions of old age as a time of fullness and lack, of continuing life and a growing attention to the unavoidability of death, that together give the film its power. The performers themselves express the film's incorporation of differences. In her discussion of the film in her memoir on its making, Mary Meigs recalls a conversation with Winifred Holden after viewing the completed film. Winnie was disappointed with the film: "Nothing happens," she said. Mary responded: "I tell her that *we* are happening. The film is about seven semiold women and a young woman happening" (qtd. in Russell 217).

---

17. I use the term "diegesis," following convention in film analysis, to refer to "the world of the film's story. The diegesis includes events that are presumed to have occurred and actions and spaces not shown onscreen" (Bordwell and Thompson 478).

In addition to the "happening" expressed in conversation and (often silent) activity, the film registers aging and time in the sequencing of static images, as the film's diegesis is repeatedly ruptured by brief photomontages that thrust viewers into self-conscious spectatorship. Each montage includes photographs of one of the seven older women at various ages. These montages are staggered throughout the film so that each is a surprise interruption of the narrative. Even more than the scenes of silent gazing that Stukator identifies, these photographic clusters disrupt the film's narrative, confronting viewers with the drastic changes of age by including images of the characters as children, young women, and mature women in quick succession. Set against the dynamic presence of the various women in the film's diegesis, these static images present viewers with the difficulty of comprehending a temporal identity that renders a subject both absent and present. These photographs function as historical traces that provide yet another identity fragment in the film, undermining the possibility of narrative totality or identity synthesis. Unnarrated, unexplained, these images are evidence of unknown histories, alerting viewers to the vast store of untold stories, the persistent mysteriousness of these characters in spite of all the audience sees and hears. Like the various strategies of representation (anecdotes and conversation, physical activity and quiet contemplation) that provide glimpses of the women as both storied subjects and opaque strangers, these "insufficient, inconclusive" photomontages (Stukator 248) remind viewers of the temporality of identity, producing paradoxical images that, in their sequencing, both halt and signify the passage of time. There is something here of Barthes's *Camera Lucida*, his famous observation of the disintegrative power of the photograph, which is "like old age: even in its splendor, it disincarnates the face, manifests its genetic evidence" (105). Barthes suggests that photographs inevitably involve comparative viewing; one sees both the image and its genetic referents, and as such, the photographic subject is always paradoxically represented and obscured. Photographs inevitably reveal the temporal subject as the image becomes a piece of comparative evidence, a single moment always referencing a multitude of others.

The photographic montages in *The Company of Strangers* are just one of the many filmic and narrative devices that engage the paradoxes and uncanniness of aging, temporality, and narrative identity. There are no narrative synopses at the film's conclusion, those common "summing up" sentences that appear after biographical and documentary films that allow us to envision lives in totality, satisfying our desires for finality. Instead, all of the women are very much *in process* at the film's end. Both the opening and final scenes depict the women in long and medium shots, walking through the misty wilderness. The mise-en-scène—that is, all that one sees within the camera's frame—provides no indication of either their origins or their destinations, and as a result the image emphasizes the activity itself, the ambulatory women *in motion*. These framing scenes of ambiguously directed movement assert in visual terms the dynamism inherent in the shouts of "We're alive!" that the women send into the darkness midway through the film. The images of movement without obvious beginning or ending provide a powerful metaphor for the uncanny selfhood produced by aging: the women are at once present and absent, in time, in space.

Perhaps more than anything, the film is a meditation on time, on the interaction of the memoried past and the active present that undermines our longing for stability. The multiple and disparate stories, images, and activities produce each character, each narrative subject, as a network, at once both teller and listener, aging and aged, subject and object. This constant fluctuation brings the women, and, I would argue, the spectator as well, into the space of Kearney's diacritical hermeneutics where subjects begin to recognize the "interconnections between the poles of sameness and strangeness" (*Strangers* 10). Such liminality can certainly be uncanny since it involves a blurring of boundaries and often the cohabitation of opposites. Age positions subjects within such a liminal space between self and other in its temporal fluidity; we are always the same and changing, ourselves and yet another. Change can be frightening, and there are many examples of aging into old age depicted as painful, if not horrifying, in popular films such as *Cocoon, Requiem for a Dream, Death Becomes Her, Whatever Happened to Baby Jane*. A film such as *The Company of Strangers*, however, provides an alternative vision of unstable, temporal identity, one without horror.

Life review typically depends on a perspective of life as a singular narrative, interpreting old age as an Eriksonian culmination that can reveal life's overall purpose. In these terms, *Shroud, The Stone Diaries*, and, to some extent, *The Stone Angel* function as problematized life review narratives in their self-reflexive interrogation of the life narrative prototype, revealing instability and multiplicity where the narrator (and often the reader) expect some teleological clarity (recall Hagar's final fragment, Axel's shifting point of view). As these interrogative life review fictions make clear, the division between evaluative, analytical review and restorative, fragmentary reminiscence is often indistinct. These four texts, *The Stone Angel, Shroud, The Stone Diaries*, and *The Company of Strangers*, depict various permutations of the project of life review, that is, the various ways one can write and read a life. In *The Stone Angel* the reflective narrator uses memory to chart a chronological past, alternating between reminiscence and present-day action, a dualist pattern that reveals a split subject struggling to negotiate between competing selves: rational and corporeal, past and present, polite and authentic. Hagar attempts to construct a metanarrative of self (albeit a self in conflict) that produces, and explains, a distinct subject moving through time in an orderly fashion. In *Shroud,* and also *The Stone Diaries,* the illusion of a unified metanarrative of self dissolves as the narrator confronts and explores the legacy of a history of poses and performance. In Banville's novel, the appropriation of various identities haunts the narrator but also potentially enlightens him, moving him toward an ethical awareness he had previously evaded. Narrative identity's fluidity, its openness to revision, becomes obvious as Axel Vander experiments with both storytelling and narrative interpretation in his exploration of his various pasts. His very name resonates with his shifting status, his pluralism. Axel is a site of change, a pivot on which various subjectivities turn, suggesting an identity at once fixed and variable.

The Company of Strangers further emphasizes this fluidity, portraying characters in the process of aging, the ongoing project of composing and revising their life narratives. These texts show how "life review" is never fully finished, or even successful, since summation and exhaustive analysis are invariably thwarted by the progress of time. These characters explore, to varying degrees, the uncanny instability produced by mortal life, which consistently replaces the singular with the multiple, the authentic self with an ever-expanding number of versions.

CHAPTER TWO

TROUBLING VERSIONS
Dementia and Identity

[M]anifestations of insanity . . . excite in the spectator the impression of automatic, mechanical processes at work behind the ordinary appearance of mental activity.

— Freud, *"The Uncanny"* 347

IN HIS personal essay documenting his father's struggle with Alzheimer's disease, Jonathan Franzen explains the necessity of his narrative intervention: "This was his disease. It was also, you could argue, his story. But you have to let me tell it" (*How to Be Alone* 11). Franzen's remarks imply the common association between lives and stories explored in chapter 1: human lives are embedded in narrative, though whether by nature (life as a linear progress toward the telos of death) or culture (a narrative-based society that influences our interpretations of aging life as a developmental "course" or "cycle") remains open to debate. But this theoretical truism, the belief that identity is based on, if not composed of, narrative, becomes problematic for those who are alienated from narrative and narration by illness and disability. Sometimes aging into old age brings disturbing changes that cannot be concealed by any facades of fixity. Later-life dementia, such as that caused by Alzheimer's, involves an alteration of the brain's physiology that results in an erosion of memory and language skills that puts incredible strain on a stable selfhood maintained by narrative. Narrative ability is greatly debilitated as victims of dementia become increasingly unable to access and employ memory in the service of language and storytelling. Narrative-based ontologies cast doubt on the continuation of selfhood in cases of dementia. As the disintegration of memory diminishes victims' narrative capability, friends and families may come to see them as strange, and even frightening, others.

Dementia is a condition that forces witnesses (family members, friends, health care providers) to respond to sufferers and the obligations they represent, a potentially crushing responsibility for another's welfare. The impossible yet necessary task of accompanying victims through the alarming disorder of their memory introduces one in painfully real terms to the exhausting demands of ethical responsibility. This is the responsibility of the witness who must, like the psychoanalyst, retain the sufferer's narrative with the hope of returning it to him or her, in an altered, mollifying form, a gift the sufferer can rarely acknowledge or even accept. Narratives of dementia inevitably involve the transfer of narrative authority to another as storytelling abilities diminish, rendering the identification of selfhood a secondary concern. More important are the issues of ethical responsibility and the politics of witnessing and testimony. The drastic changes imposed by dementia expose the radical impermanence of our temporal condition. Though it is certainly true that many people who age into old age will not suffer from dementia, awareness of its debilitating power casts a heavy shadow over our apprehensions of aging. The aversion to dementia provokes Christine Cassel, former president of the American College of Physicians, to label "dementing illness . . . the single most powerful factor in the negative attitudes about aging that occur in our society and throughout the world. . . . The stereotype of the elderly person as inevitably 'losing it' is an enormous barrier to progress in productive aging" (x). As a primary source of the overriding dread of old age, dementia is an age-related disability that demands inquiry.

MEMORY AND FORGETTING

Cognitive science teaches that memory is unstable, even in physiological terms. The past is at least partly created by one's recollections since memories are, in a sense, both strengthened and altered by the very act of remembering. Neurological models of memory can help to confirm the unavoidable nonfixity of the memoried past, revealing how the recollection of an event is simultaneously the construction of an event (Eakin, *Making Selves* 106). To a certain degree, the past serves the subject's narrative purposes. As Eakin remarks in his study of autobiography and identity, "students of memory today hold that past experience is necessarily—both psychologically and neurologically—*constructed* anew in each memory event or act of recall. Memories, then, are constructed, and memory itself, moreover, is plural" (107, original emphasis). According to these models, memories are often "actually memories of memories" (Franzen, *How to Be Alone* 27), rather than memories of an actual experience.

Jonathan Franzen draws on recent neurological research to explain how the "brain is not an album in which memories are stored discretely like unchanging photographs"; instead, each memory is an "approximate excitation of neural circuits that bind a set of sensory images and semantic data into the momentary sensation of a remembered whole. These images and data are seldom the exclusive property of one particular memory" (Franzen 8). As a result, memories are largely interconnected and easily triggered by excitation of related regions of the brain, forming a "constellation" that is preserved through the very act of remembering. Memories must be recalled to remain memories, since "each succeeding recollection and retelling reinforces the constellation of images and knowledge that constitute the memory. At the cellular level, according to neuroscientists, I'm burning the memory in a little deeper each time, strengthening the dendritic connections among its components, further encouraging the firing of that specific set of synapses" (Franzen 9). In these terms, narrative is not simply the emplotment of memory; memory itself is created by its telling. Storytelling at once confirms and even creates memory, since that which is not repeatedly recalled is easily lost. A useful image for considering the action of memory is the palimpsest, a continually reinscribed parchment upon which each recollected text supersedes the previous one. Palimpsestic memory involves endlessly recalled and retold narratives that inevitably obscure the supposedly original recollected experience. As a result, remembering and telling the past at once recapture and replace what came before, in effect dissolving the previous memory. The process of endless substitution involved in the very mechanics of memory calls into question the simple, intuitive expectation of correlation between one's memory of a thing and the thing itself. Instead, memory is itself an unstable process in which connections are easily and continuously modified.

The other side of this substitutive memorial process is the larger, constant action of forgetting. Almost everything in one's life remains unremembered, a phenomenon both remarkable and unsettling. This "great adaptive [virtue] of our brains, [that is] our ability to forget almost everything that has ever happened to us," dooms us to unavoidable but necessary loss (Franzen, *How to Be Alone* 9). Herbert Blau finds this unstoppable forgetting responsible for the frequent unfulfillment experienced as one enters later life: "there is . . . a perturbation of aging that comes, just over the threshold of consciousness from want of consciousness, a last sad intimation of the life we've never lived because essentially unremembered, so that there is a sense of having suffered somehow an irreparable loss that, because not known, we cannot even mourn" (Blau 34). Such profound forgetting is tied to the uncanny in its referencing of the absent. We do not know what we have forgotten (almost all of our daily actions since birth), yet we know that we have forgotten. The remarkable persistence of forgetting, though essential for day-to-day functioning, means that subjects are always haunted by "intimations of the life we've never lived."

Dementia is a pathological experience of the unsettling forgotten life. And it is here, I argue, that fiction and filmmaking step in, representational arts at once preserving and mourning what has been lost. Perhaps dementia—an inevitable process of forgetting and loss—is a grotesque exaggeration of what human temporality, our condition as aging subjects, enacts. The very terminology of "remembering" points to its corrective force: "Etymology tells us that to remember is to 'piece together,' to 'recollect' is to gather again what has been lost. In this sense, memory is always recuperative, restorative, an act of reclamation" (Small 64). The term "recollect" has an even more obvious restorative function. One re-collects that which has been scattered; remembering inevitably grapples with loss.

Narrative identity involves a complex matrix of self that includes experience, storytelling, and story-listening. As explored in the previous chapter, Ricoeur understands selfhood as a telling-effect:[1] "Our own existence cannot be separated from the account we can give of ourselves. It is in telling our own stories that we give ourselves an identity. We recognize ourselves in the stories that we tell about ourselves. It makes very little difference whether these stories are true or false, fiction as well as verifiable history provides us with an identity" (qtd. in Kerby 40–41). Kerby expands the claim, suggesting that identity is formed as much by our own storytelling as by our appearance as "a character" in other people's narratives (40). The inseparability of existing as a person and telling stories of that existence implies that those unable to tell their stories face serious

---

1. I borrow this terminology from Paul John Eakin, whose article in the journal *Narrative* explores identity according to cognitive science models. In particular he uses the work of Antonia Damasio to argue that "instead of a teller, there is only—and persistently—what we might call a *teller-effect*, a self that emerges and lives its life only within the narrative matrix of consciousness" ("What Are We Reading" 129, emphasis added).

impediments to functioning as subjects.[2] The person unable to articulate his or her stories is no less a subject but is increasingly dependent on others to assist in narrativization, in review and interpretation. Is a subject unable to tell his or her stories not a self? Can others tell the victim's stories without a loss of that victim's selfhood? Considering these questions can contribute to a better understanding of the function and consequences of the narrative problems that often occur in later life.

AGING AND DEMENTIA

Unfortunately, medical research suggests that merely aging into old age seriously increases one's risk of developing dementia—most commonly as a result of Alzheimer's disease or vascular dementia (see Rockwood and Lindesay 6). Many of the extreme impairments (acute confusion, hallucinations) associated with dementia fall under the category of delirium—indeed the two conditions are often difficult to distinguish, and age is also a primary risk factor for delirium (Rockwood and Lindesay 5–6). In fact, researchers claim that "late-onset Alzheimer's disease and vascular dementia appeared to have a stronger association with delirium than did early-onset Alzheimer's disease and frontotemporal dementia" (Lindesay, Rockwood, and Rolfson 38–39). According to the Alzheimer's Association, "increasing age is the greatest risk factor for Alzheimer's. One in 10 individuals over 65 and nearly half over 85 are affected" ("Fact Sheet: Alzheimer's Disease Statistics"; see also Sabat).

The difficulty of narrativizing dementia draws attention to the relation between experience, or the raw "material" of narrative, and the mimetic project of representing that material. As discussed earlier, the relationship between events of the supposed real world and their narrative emplotment is a vexed one. Counter to commonsensical notions of narrative representation, narrative theorists demonstrate that the interaction between events and their narrative presentation may be less discrete than they first appear. The relationship between narrative and identity works much like the

2. My work on this chapter has shown me that "caregiving" is a highly complicated response to witnessing. In this chapter I limit my discussion to caregiving provided by children and spouses, though I realize that much of the responsibility for the welfare of dementia victims falls on various professional caregivers, including doctors, nurses, and home health aides. Financial remuneration triangulates the patient/caregiver dyad by introducing the figure of the remunerator, an alteration with serious repercussions for the theorization of responsibility and obligation.

"double logic" theory of narrative that Porter Abbott takes from Jonathan Culler. Within this model, "story appears both to precede *and* to come after narrative discourse" (Abbott, *Narrative* 18, original emphasis).[3] By substituting the term "identity" for "story," one sees clearly the paradox of narrative identity in which presentation appears as *re*-presentation, formulation as illustration; in other words, when subjects tell stories about themselves they are creating selves. The "I" expressed via narrative cannot exist without this narrative apparatus, and the narrative apparatus is predicated upon the "I" subject.

By extension, the question of whether identity is located in embodied experience or in its narrative communication is pre-empted by objections to such a division itself. Certainly, self-*understanding* seems to be the result of storytelling, drawing the other into one's experience of self: "We accept that we are narrative beings because the shortest road from self to self is through the other" (Kearney, *Strangers* 231). The reduced self-understanding available to victims of dementia is one of many ways that sufferers become dependent on others. In cases of dementia, storytelling does not necessarily disappear, but the narratives that remain become increasingly opaque to listeners, consisting often of noncontextualized narrative fragments or even nonsense. As a result, understanding becomes increasingly collaborative for sufferers of dementia. As Franzen reminds his readers, it is his father's story; but we must let the son tell it. As the many caregiver support groups make clear, diseases such as Alzheimer's place grave demands on caregivers,[4] not least of which is assisting sufferers in their

3. Culler's explication of "a certain self-deconstructive force in narrative and the theory of narrative" reveals how story (the events that purportedly make up a narrative) and discourse (the presentation of events) are not as discrete as narratologists would like (187). "Analysis of narrative depends . . . on the distinction between story and discourse, and this distinction always involves a relation of dependency. . . . Since the distinction between story and discourse can function only if there is a determination of one by the other, the analyst must always choose which will be treated as the given and which as the product" (186). Culler argues that both the assumption that discourse is the presentation of a pre-existing story and that the belief that "'events' are nothing other than products of discourse" blind critics to the double logic of story and discourse (186). His analysis has interesting parallels with narrative identity: as simultaneous reader and writer of his or her stories, the subject at once shapes and is shaped by narrative.

4. Eva Kittay's work on the ethics of care emphasizes the needs and dependencies that result from caregiving, stressing the "nested dependencies" that result from human interdependence. She champions the notion of "*doulia*," shifting the original Greek definition of servant or slave to a more reciprocal meaning, using the term to "signify instead a caregiver who cares for those who care for others" (107). According to

negotiation of an unremembered, nonnarrative, and, consequently, largely incomprehensible existence.

The collaborative dimensions of the caregiver-patient relationship demonstrate the potential of assisted identity, the possibility that dementia might diminish the chasm between self and other, enforcing a subjectivity of exchange. This is counterintuitive since, as the many victims of dementia know (here I refer to both the afflicted and those who care for them), much of the pain of dementia comes from its alienating effect. The opportunities for communication and understanding are seriously diminished. But it is these very difficulties that may increase the potential for, indeed may enforce, ethical insight in the caregiver. I argue that dementia often forces its responsive witnesses into a Levinasian interaction with the other. In their exaggerated otherness, victims of dementia demand an unfulfillable responsibility, and caregivers experience in everyday terms the difficulty, often the impossibility, of responding to the basic obligation that the other represents. According to Levinas, the other takes the self "hostage," but it is this position of subordination that is necessary for ethical relations: "It is through the condition of being hostage that there can be in the world pity, compassion, pardon and proximity—even the little there is, even the simple 'After you, sir.' The unconditionality of being hostage is not the limit case of solidarity, but the condition for all solidarity" (*Otherwise* 17). In an interview with Richard Kearney, Levinas further explained the restructuring of identity that is concomitant with ethical awareness: "The ethical exigency to be responsible for the other undermines the ontological primacy of the meaning of being; it unsettles the natural and political positions we have taken up in the world and predisposes us to a meaning that is other than being, that is otherwise than being (*autrement qu'être*)" (23). Later-life dementia often has such a rattling effect, enforcing a kind of Levinasian subordination with ontological implications for both witnesses and sufferers.

Because narratives of dementia are unavoidably collaborative, there is the potential in these narratives for the victim to be more than simply strange, more than a pathological object. An ethical, empathetic interaction can reveal the "patient" as in fact an uncanny subject, an exaggerated embodiment of difference, of radical impermanence. Dementia provides caregivers, storytellers, with dramatic lessons on uncanny identity. Not

---

Kittay's "principle of *doulia*," "*Just as we have required care to survive and thrive, so we need to provide conditions that allow others—including those who do the work of caring—to receive the care they need to survive and thrive*" (107, original emphasis).

only is there the obvious uncanniness of the victim whose deteriorated memory produces a frightening strangeness, but there is often self-revelation for the storyteller who comes to recognize his or her own otherness in the process of collaborating with the afflicted.

The power of narrative to alter perspective is central to theories of empathy: catharsis allows us to experience the suffering of others "*as if* we were them. . . . And it is exactly this double-take of difference and identity—experiencing oneself as another and the other as oneself—that provokes a reversal of our natural attitude to things and opens us to novel ways of seeing and being" (Kearney, *On Stories* 140). This vision of narrative catharsis echoes the uncanny in its pattern of reversals and double vision. Indeed, Royle characterizes the very acts of writing and reading as unavoidably uncanny: "One tries to keep oneself out, but one cannot. One tries to put oneself in: same result. The uncanny is an experience of being after oneself, in various senses of that phrase" (16). I propose that narratives of dementia accentuate these uncanny and cathartic, even uncannily cathartic, potentials of narrative. As I have tried to demonstrate, old age and, more specifically, narratives of old age are involved in this process of revelation, since aging into old age exposes temporality and the concomitant instability of selfhood. Narratives of late-life dementia, such as that caused by Alzheimer's disease, exaggerate this revelation, exposing the radical instability of temporal identity and the ethical demands it initiates.

TELLING OTHER PEOPLE'S STORIES

Dementia is such a disturbing sign of disease largely because it denies sufferers the ability to "be themselves" as they lose their memory and, therefore, their stories. As a result, the subjective experience of dementia, particularly of its late stages, remains largely unknown since it destroys precisely those tools necessary to produce a coherent life story.[5] What do exist, however, are narratives by the survivors of dementia, that is, stories (in both memoirs and fiction) told by caregivers that speak to the ethical crises provoked by the condition, the difficulty of assisting a person who often cannot acknowledge, or perhaps even tolerate, help.[6] Though subjec-

5. I have come across a few first-person accounts of the disease: *Losing My Mind: An Intimate Look at Life with Alzheimer's*, by Thomas DeBaggio; and *My Journey into Alzheimer's Disease*, by Robert Davis. The latter includes material written by the author's wife, Betty, continuing the trend of witnesses speaking for the afflicted.

6. There are a number of nonfictional memoirs written by witnesses. A sampling

tive depictions of dementia are often impossible, fiction can provide an imaginative construction of dementia. But even those that offer an inside view, as it were, of the disease can go only so far. The dark final stages of dementia may be beyond the reach of representation or imagination. Novels such as Mordecai Richler's *Barney's Version,* Jonathan Franzen's *The Corrections,* and Jeffrey Moore's *The Memory Artists,* which present compelling self-portraits of dementia in fiction narrated or focalized by victims of the condition, are unable to continue this fictional conceit into the later stages of disorientation. The deterioration of language skills is an insurmountable obstacle to linguistic communication. In all instances the writers overcome this obstacle by transferring the narration to a caregiving child.[7]

The practice of telling other people's stories has its own difficult politics. An ethical relationship between teller and subject, particularly in cases involving dementia and other memory disorders, depends on a careful balance of empathy and respect, a conscientious negotiation of the difficult terrain between outright rejection and debilitating identification. The problem posed by subjects unable to tell their stories has been considered by many critics; in particular, trauma theorists have explored the complicated interrelationship of witnessing and testimonial, empathy and identification.[8] There are important differences between trauma and dementia, the most prominent being the source of the condition as situational or biological. Sufferers of Alzheimer's, Parkinson's, or vascular dementia, for example, have little to no capacity to control their condition, since their memories become physiologically unavailable as the brain is devastated by the disease. But there are similarities in the symptoms of trauma and dementia: involuntary repetition, confusion, hallucination, and of course

---

of titles includes *Remind Me Who I Am, Again,* by Linda Grant; *The House on Beartown Road: A Memoir of Learning and Forgetting,* by Elizabeth Cohen; *The Story of My Father,* by Sue Miller; *Dancing on Quicksand: A Gift of Friendship in the Age of Alzheimer's,* by Marilyn Mitchell; and *Do You Remember Me?: A Father, a Daughter, and a Search for the Self,* by Judith Levine.

7. Interestingly, in all three examples it is a son who provides the primary (narrative) care, regardless of the sex of the victim, a reversal of demographic trends, which confirm that care providers are actually predominantly women. A quick survey of the texts that make up the bulk of this chapter reveals a continuation of this reversal, men caring for afflicted loved ones, both male and female, the only exception being Alice Munro's "Spelling." The preponderance of male caregivers and the gendered implications of dementia are issues I return to in the chapter's conclusion.

8. I refer here primarily to the work of Cathy Caruth, Shoshona Felman, Geoffrey Hartman, Dominick LaCapra, and Dori Laub.

memory loss. Both conditions inhibit communication and result in the disappearance of memories that may re-emerge unexpectedly, though this is more likely in cases of psychological trauma. As a result, trauma theory has something to offer an analysis of narratives of dementia, particularly in its theorization of witnessing and testimonial, and the potentials and perils of telling other people's stories.

To a large extent the sufferer of dementia is unable to give testimony, a narrative process that Dori Laub has described as essential for restoring the past to the victim of trauma (69–70). Pathological memory disorders such as Alzheimer's work in the opposite way to psychological trauma. Inconceivable horrors such as those suffered by victims of the Holocaust can only be witnessed "belatedly" as a result of "human cognitive capacity to perceive and to assimilate the totality of what was really happening at the time" (Laub 69). Dementia reverses this process of revelation as sufferers' testimonial potential, their ability to act as witnesses to their own experiences, lessens over time. Laub describes the important role of the "interviewer-listener" in Holocaust testimonial, his or her "responsibility for bearing witness that previously the narrator felt he [or she] bore alone, and therefore could not carry out. It is the encounter and the coming together between the survivor and the listener that makes possible something like a repossession of the act of witnessing" (69). This kind of reciprocal collaboration is often not possible for victims of dementia; indeed, the very language of the "survivor" is incongruous since later-life dementia is typically the result of a fatal disease, the most prominent being Alzheimer's.

Though there can be no "survivors" of Alzheimer's, testimony remains important, the responsibility of witnessing transferred onto caregivers, who are most often family members, typically spouses or children of the afflicted. Witnessing is a serious responsibility that involves a difficult integration of past and present narratives, an integration the afflicted cannot manage. The dialogic aspects of testimony and witnessing become increasingly difficult to sustain as dementia worsens and the victim's narrative speech becomes incomprehensible, or even unavailable. Traditional efforts at witnessing trauma involve "facing loss," those losses too terrible for comprehension that refuse to inhabit only the past, persisting instead as ghosts that haunt the victim. For victims of dementia and their caregivers, loss is a continual process, and the future can promise only further debilitation and disappearance. Dementia often produces what Felman calls "*involuntary witness[es],*" reluctant caregivers forced to observe the dissolution of their loved one (Felman and Laub 4, original emphasis).

"The contemporary writer," argues Felman, "often dramatizes the predicament (whether chosen or imposed, whether conscious or unconscious) of a voluntary or of an unwitting, inadvertent, and sometimes *involuntary witness:* witness to a trauma, to a crime or to an outrage; witness to a horror or an illness whose effects explode any capacity for explanation or rationalization" (4, original emphasis). Felman explicitly connects the compulsion to witness and testify with the mortal threat of disease: "what alerts and mobilizes the attention of the witness and what necessitates the testimony is always fundamentally, in one way or another, the scandal of an illness, of a metaphorical or literal disease" (4–5). Contemporary fiction dealing with the frightening trauma of later-life dementia grapples with the difficult, even dangerous, interaction of the afflicted and his or her witness. Such illness tests the limits of witnessing and testimonial—how does one ethically listen when the sufferer is no longer able to testify? Later-life dementia forces the witness into a position of interpreter that complicates a common association of the witness with truth-finding and the preservation of history. Witnessing and testimonial inevitably involve exchange, a blending of perspectives and stories as witnesses become involved in the testimony they receive. As mediums, witnesses become collaborators, and in cases of dementia such participation often becomes increasingly active. Merely listening becomes inadequate when the victim can no longer use language to tell stories; at such a point the roles bleed into one another: the caregiver provides the testimony the victim can no longer formulate. As Franzen writes of his father, "It was . . . his story. But you have to let me tell it." It may be the case that the very act of witnessing is unavoidably involved in integration and transgression: "The witness . . . testifies to what has been said *through* him. Because the witness has said 'here I am' before the other" (Levinas qtd. in Felman 3, original emphasis). Later-life dementia may disrupt the discrete categories of witness and other. The witness is a medium, but often an originating speaker as well, forced to salvage, repair, sustain, and even create narratives that have been damaged or erased.

The potential for collaborative understanding is part of the ethical potential of literary and film narrative practice as an illuminating exchange between self and other that allows readers and viewers to glimpse their own difference. As discussed above, Kearney privileges narrative-induced empathy as a highly productive and redemptive goal, as the primary means for attaining ethical human interaction (*On Stories* 62–63). Likewise, Ann Whitehead characterizes narrative exchange as an "ethical practice," particularly in trauma studies, that works to "return to the patient his or her own story" (8). Returning a story often means speaking *for* the patient, a ventriloquism that requires constant vigilance. As Amy Shuman advises, such storytelling easily slips from appropriation into exploitation, creating "voyeurs rather than witnesses," who often "foreclose meaning rather than open lines of inquiry and understanding" (5). Shuman proposes "a critique of empathy" to combat such foreclosure, a critique that recognizes the risks of adopting and retelling the stories of others by demanding "obligations between tellers, listeners, and the stories they borrow" (5). In addition to the problem of voyeurism and exploitative appropriation is the danger of overidentification with the victim, an intensification of empathy that puts the witness at risk (LaCapra 212–13). Consequently, witnessing, and telling victims' stories, is a delicate operation that demands negotiation between too little and too much sympathy, between observation and participation. Narratives of dementia rehearse this balancing act in their representations of victims and caregivers collaborating and exchanging roles. The depictions of dementia included in this chapter show the strain of maintaining ethical empathy and the many risks to self involved in witnessing the transformation of a loved one into an uncanny specter. This distressing vision—the victim is totally other, yet undeniably familiar, known for decades as husband or father, wife or mother—is a witnessing of aging, temporality, difference, that can activate a reluctant, and often disturbing, insight into the uncanniness of selfhood.

DEMENTIA AND NARRATIVE
Barney's Version and Iris

In many ways, Mordecai Richler's novel *Barney's Version* forms a bridge between the previous chapter's focus on life review and my current attention to narratives of dementia. Written in the first person, *Barney's Version* is just that, the narrator's *version* of his life story, a narrative complicated by his worsening Alzheimer's. Barney Panofsky insists that his version is the authentic one, representing "this shambles that is the true story of my wasted life" (1), in opposition to the slanderous version of Barney Panofsky offered in his enemy Terry McIver's memoir. Barney regards narrative as a redemptive restoration of truth that will order the chaos of his life, "retrieve some sense" and "unscrambl[e] it" (26). But his narrative is plagued by memory slips that frustrate his efforts at clear, redemptive prose. Barney's difficulties with memory and language assert themselves from the novel's beginning:

> Hold the phone. I'm stuck. I'm trying to remember the name of the author
> of *The Man in the Gray Flannel Suit.* Or was it *The Man in the Brooks
> Brothers Shirt?* No, that was written by a fibber. Lillian what's-her-name?
> Come on. I know it. Like the mayonnaise. Lillian Kraft? No. *Hellman.*
> *Lillian Hellman.* The name of the author of *The Man in the Gray Flannel
> Suit* doesn't matter. It's of no importance. But now that it's started I won't
> sleep tonight. (10–11)

Indeed, as he is falling asleep that night, the sudden absence of vocabulary
confronts him again when he finds himself unable to "remember the name
of the thing you use to strain spaghetti" (11). The narrative is littered with
such self-conscious struggles with memory, the increasing inaccessibility of
language. Early on, Barney develops a series of slogans designed to return
fugitive vocabulary to its proper place. These phrases come to function as
an assertion of self, creating a list of stable, authentic knowledge meant to
ward off the frightening and unavoidable changes of later-life dementia:

> I began to mutter what is becoming my mantra. Spaghetti is strained with
> the device I have hanging on my kitchen wall. Mary McCarthy wrote
> *The Man in the Brooks Brothers Suit.* Or *Shirt.* Whichever. I am once a
> widower and twice divorced. I have three children—Michael, Kate, and
> the other boy. My favourite dish is braised brisket with horseradish and
> latkes. Miriam is my heart's desire. I live on Sherbrooke Street West in
> Montreal. The street number doesn't matter, I'd know the building any-
> where. (88)

In his struggle to preserve the details of his identity, Barney mixes the
everyday with the intimate, making the function and location of a col-
ander equally important as his feelings for his ex-wife, Miriam, and the
names of his children. Barney's compulsive rehearsal of these "life facts"
functions as a metaphor of the larger narrative, the anxious narration of
details meant to shore up a faltering identity. The two acts of storytelling,
micro and macro, point to Barney's narration as a project of preservation,
an undertaking that grows increasingly difficult as his illness worsens.

In *Barney's Version,* narrative is self-consciously delivered as a manifestation of self, an authentic riposte to the deceptions of McIver's narrative.
Even beyond identity *representation,* Barney's effort to tell "the true story
of my wasted life" is an effort at identity *construction,* an effort to produce
a "true" self via a "true story" (52). But as the narrative proceeds, the spu-
riousness of his project becomes evident. Even the singular "version" of

the novel's title suggests the existence of alternatives, alerting readers to the fact that this story is in fact only one subject's telling of a tale, undermining the ostensibly definitive nature of this "true story." Writing of the Borges's story, "The Garden of Forking Paths," Porter Abbott describes the dense narrative web that constantly surrounds the subject, the idea that "from one moment to the next any person inhabits an infinitude of potential stories, any one of which may or may not intersect with any one of the infinitude inhabited by anyone else" ("The Future" 530). Barney's narrative points to the "infinitude" of stories lying outside his personal version. The inclusion of (fictional) textual apparatuses, such as brief excerpts from enemy Terry McIver's journals, newspaper articles, and son Michael Panofsky's footnotes and afterword, situates Barney's narrative as fragmentary, as one text of many. In particular, Michael's footnotes and afterword,[9] ostensibly necessitated by Barney's Alzheimer's-related narrative difficulties, place Barney in a larger narrative web that emphasizes multiplicity: Barney is at once the dynamic, persuasive subject guiding the bulk of the novel, the by turns frustrating, charming, pathetic character in the anecdotal stories provided by his wife and children, and the pathological object alienated by mental disorder.

Unwittingly collaborative, Barney's narrative is in fact completed by others; indeed, the novel's central mystery is solved by Michael, a deduction that finally abolishes the specter of criminality that has darkened Barney's narrative. As a result, the novel poses serious questions regarding the ethics of representation, in particular, the ethics of telling another's stories. The novel presents an interpretative dilemma: the reader can regard Barney as the only legitimate voice of authority, making the novel's appara-

---

9. Michael Panofsky's rational afterword, which contains and explains the intimate, and often painful, personal narrative supplied by Barney, exposes an imbalance of power that echoes the relations of self and other in other categories of difference, for example, race. In some ways Panofsky's additions recall the function and effect of the emendations white abolitionists often made to slave narratives. Such textual apparatuses sought to legitimize and interpret the slave narrative, often underscoring the pathos of the tale in order to stir the reader to action. In other words, emendations such as the preface to *Narrative of the Life of Frederick Douglass, An American Slave* by William Lloyd Garrison delimit textual meaning, employing the slave narrative as a tool of agitation: "Reader! are you with the man-stealers in sympathy and purpose, or on the side of their down-trodden victims?" (Garrison 42). Such bracketing apparatuses contain and often overwrite the voice of the subaltern, even as they seek to increase its efficacy. My interpretation of Michael Panofsky's additions in *Barney's Version* also highlights a contradictory effect, arguing that his afterword at once objectifies and redeems the subjectivity it replaces.

tus, son Michael's afterword and footnotes, violations of that authority; or one can regard the two narrators as collaborators, interpreting Michael's narration as an ethical act of continuation that redeems his father, saving him from some of the dissolutions of dementia. Though often laughably pedantic, in the case of the footnotes, or painfully descriptive, in the case of the afterword, Michael's narration alerts the reader to the multiplicity of interpretations, the proliferation of "versions" that Barney's story threatens to deny in its "life review" model. In the novel's final pages, narrated by Michael, comes the realization that Bernard (Boogie) Moscovitch's disappearance, a vanishing that resulted in Barney's trial for murder, was actually caused by an unlikely accident involving a water bomber. Consequently, it is Michael's act of speaking *for*, as well as about, his father that restores Barney's innocence. Michael's appropriation of narrative voice enacts a redemption unavailable to Barney himself. As well, the afterword in some sense "saves" Barney's narrative, at least in generic terms, providing the satisfying resolution demanded of any mystery story. Not only does Michael's narration rescue Barney from the role of murderer, but it also serves to position Barney in a larger narrative web, showing how his stories interconnect with those of others. The afterword necessitated by the dissolution of Barney's storytelling abilities serves to redeem and preserve his narrative and, consequently, his identity.

Though the novel concludes with Barney still alive, he is in what Michael calls a "near-vegetable state" (416). Michael's depiction of debilitated Barney is at odds with the preceding four-hundred-page life review. These adjacent narratives effect a kind of disorienting double vision: Barney appears at once as subject (as blustering storyteller) and object (as debilitated patient). Such double vision destabilizes the discourse of definitive versions, definitive selves, affording the reader a glimpse of identity as change and contradiction, what Abbott calls "the *frisson* of gathering indeterminacies" ("The Future" 530). What *Barney's Version* accomplishes is a revision of the discourse of singularity, revealing any story, any life narrative, as merely *a* version within a larger, shifting narrative network. Michael's narration intimates the existence of nonlinguistic subjectivity, portraying Barney in his disability, unable to speak or write, but wishing to dance. The narration intimates his continuing emotional life, evident in his gestures and expressions, but such reactions are no longer explained. The reader witnesses Barney only from the outside now, glimpsing the otherness that his first-person life review had obscured. Richler's novel reveals how the effects of Alzheimer's disease mark the uncanny instability of human identity, our status as temporal beings.

As Ricoeur and other narrative theorists insist, there is always another version, another story (*Time* 3: 249). But even such multiplicity depends on self-awareness as subjects "recognize themselves in the stories they tell about themselves" (*Time* 3: 247), a process of identification that collapses in the face of dementia, which seriously obstructs, if not destroys, a person's ability to narrate and recognize. In the following chapter on the double, I deal with problems surrounding visual recognition in more detail, but for the remainder of this chapter, I explore the identity crises that emerge out of the pathological destruction of memory in old age. Richard Eyre's film *Iris,* along with fiction by Munro and Franzen, demonstrates how later-life dementia lays bare the confounding otherness of the other, a strangeness made all the more bizarre by the traces of familiarity that remain. Dementia forces loved ones to become caregivers and narrative collaborators who must attend to the impossible demands of the uncanny sufferer. The caregiver often confronts the difficulty of narrative communication while at the same time respecting the limits of what he or she continues to offer, typically narrative fragments, incongruous phrases, along with the nonlexical pleasures of embodiment, the pleasures of food and drink, swimming, dancing, or singing. Later-life dementia forces a caregiver to step back from the illusory oneness of love to rediscover the insurmountable twoness of the couple. In his interview with Kearney, Levinas comments on the "platonic ontology" of the romantic tradition, arguing that "[m]an's relationship with the other is *better* as difference than as unity: sociality is better than fusion. The very value of love is the impossibility of reducing the other to myself, of coinciding into sameness" (22). But the pathological difference of dementia can effectively cancel the value of love's irreducibility as otherness tips over into pathology. Such a painful glimpse of the loved one's strangeness can haunt the caregiver, overwhelming him or her with the uncanny experience of witnessing the exposure of absolute otherness, recalling the epigraph's attention to the uncanny "impression of automatic, mechanical processes at work behind the ordinary appearance of mental activity." Levinas reflects on the consequences of recognizing otherness and the responsibility it entails: "As soon as I acknowledge that it is 'I' who am responsible, I accept that my freedom is anteceded by an obligation to the other. Ethics redefines subjectivity as this heteronomous responsibility, in contrast to autonomous freedom. . . . The other haunts our ontological existence and keeps the psyche awake, in a state of vigilant insomnia" (27–28). The language of haunting is pertinent here, pointing to the destabilizing effect of witnessing the other. The caregivers in these narratives are all haunted in various ways, their stable identities shaken by new insights into the transformative effects of aging and dementia.[10]

Though lacking the intimacy of *Barney's Version*'s first-person narrator, the biographical film *Iris* demonstrates in a different register the unavoidability of narrative appropriation in cases of late-life dementia. Based on Iris Murdoch's husband John Bayley's memoirs, *Iris: A Memoir* and *Elegy for Iris*, the film is a portrait of the novelist Iris Murdoch, in particular her late-life struggles with Alzheimer's disease. In many ways, *Iris* is similar to the film *The Notebook*, discussed in the introduction. Both films involve an older couple whose love is strained and strengthened by the older woman's dementia. Like *The Notebook*, *Iris* is structured according to the dualism of young versus old, with images of the old, debilitated Iris set against those of the young, vivacious Iris. The viewer witnesses little of Iris Murdoch's process of aging into old age; indeed, only one brief episode during the film's introductory intercutting between past and present depicts an older Iris still fully in control of memory and language, despite the fact that Bayley's memoir *Elegy for Iris* claims the impairments of Alzheimer's were not obvious until Iris was in her seventies. In *Iris* old age is dramatized primarily as a descent into pathology as Iris succumbs to the debilitations of dementia.

From early on, the film contrasts vital youth with fading age. Viewers' second glimpse of old Iris (Judi Dench)[11] is not of one of "her," at least not in her entirety. A close-up shows her wrinkled hand in the act of writing with a blue pen. The hand jots down a few words before pausing and the camera tilts up to provide a close-up of old Iris's grave profile, an image of intellectual and bodily suspension; her hand paused midsentence is either an instance or a foreshadowing of Alzheimer's impairments. The caging frame of the image echoes the neurological restrictions closing in on old Iris. A sound bridge introduces images of an energetic, happy

---

10. The narratives I examine repeatedly collapse the two conditions, figuring old age and pathology as indistinguishable demonstrations of painful mortality. For example, in both the Munro stories I discuss, there is never any mention of disease; rather, the debilitating disorientation and forgetfulness experienced by the characters Fiona and Flo appear distinctly linked to their advanced age. Though Alfred's dementia in *The Corrections* is the result of Parkinson's disease, the narration often associates his age and pathology: "The sight of Alfred's suddenly aged face, its disintegration-in-progress, its redness and asymmetries, cut Chip like a bullwhip" (541). Here age is one of Alfred's diseases.

11. In order to avoid confusion I differentiate characters as young or old, a naming I believe echoes the film's binaristic model of identity. Therefore, Kate Winslet's character is "young Iris," Judi Dench's is "old Iris," and so on.

past. The film cuts to a long shot of dynamic young Iris (Kate Winslet) zooming along a country road through lush green forests on her bicycle. "Iris! Iris, wait for me," young John Bayley (Hugh Bonneville) pleads, his bicycle trailing behind hers. "Just keep tight hold of me and it'll be all right," she answers. "You won't keep still," he complains. Young Iris's response evokes the fervent energy of youth: "I can't keep still," she calls back to him. In this brief cycling sequence, the wideframing gives Winslet ample room to move, unlike the amputating extreme close-up of old Iris's hand, her strained expression, framing that fragments the figure and inhibits movement. As the effects of Alzheimer's quickly become apparent in the film's first act (the symptoms include the repetition of phrases, sudden bursts into song, a failure to recognize familiars), the mise-en-scène further directs the viewer's interpretation of the present, and by implication, old age. The vibrant colors and warm, soft light of young Iris's world contrast sharply with the increasingly dull hues and dim dusty light of old Iris's greatly circumscribed and cluttered spaces, a visual differentiation that continues throughout the film. Indeed, locations, such as the English seaside, are signaled as either past or present by their lighting. Here age appears as a literal dimming that leaves the protagonist shuffling through disordered, shadowy spaces.

In this differentiation the editing and mise-en-scène reinforce cultural scripts of aging by dividing the lifecourse into the diametrically opposed categories of young and old,[12] a practice of segmentation that signals what Woodward labels our "curious arithmetical relation to time. In this sense, the unconscious could be said to be able to count only up to two" (*Discontents* 184–85). But aging into old age often erodes this binarism, with uncanny results. The changes of age may involve an intrusion of time's otherness, a glimpse of the nonarithmetical that undermines categorization. Though *Iris* polarizes human life into categories of old and young, it also evokes continuity, a blurring of boundaries that exposes age as uncannily fluid and nonlinear. Furthermore, the film simultaneously sympathizes with the pathos of Iris's illness, elegizing the gradual erasure of her memory and abilities, and actually contributes to such erasure, substituting one version for many: the undoubtedly abundant narratives that constitute Iris the writer, Iris the mature, accomplished woman, Iris the public intellectual, are overwritten with narratives of illness and loss. As such, the film threatens to transform Iris Murdoch into a mascot for dementia.[13]

---

12. This temporal binarism mimics the organization of Bayley's *Elegy for Iris*, which is split into two sections, titled "Then" and "Now."

13. The paratextual apparatus included on the DVD attests to this mascot status.

In *Iris* the disruption of temporal polarization (the dividing of Iris into young and old) suggests an experience of nonarithmetical time. The film's editing brings temporal spaces together, occasionally allowing past and present, young and old to occupy the same frame, or at least the same narrative sequence. The film uses connective editing techniques, particularly eyeline matches and a concluding match on action,[14] to intermingle past and present, thereby admitting the familiarity so lacking in the mise-en-scène's radical differentiation between the warm past and chilly present. The fluidity suggested by the editing prevents young Iris and young John from being entirely estranged from old Iris and old John, depicting a continuity that encourages the viewer to recognize these characters as the same, but different, persons, demonstrating how the familiar introduced into the strange can provoke the uncanny. The film clouds and complicates the discrete categories of young and old by attending to continuity, suggesting the constancy of aging that makes subjects always other than themselves, endlessly different, yet the same. In *Iris*, editorial choices produce ripples in the dyad of "then" and "now."

Indeed, the film uses water imagery to underscore the fluid interpenetration of temporal spaces. The title credits appear over an underwater sequence that is hazy, yet gentle, the cloudy river water shot through with wavering beams of sunshine. Underwater plants brush past the camera's lens as it moves forward through the murky water. The extradiegetic music of pulsing strings is hushed yet expectant. A shadowy shape enters the corner of the frame accompanied by a celebratory shimmer of cymbals. A naked young Iris swims by the camera, and the title appears transposed over the nymphlike image. Young John enters the frame and moves toward her; they join hands and move toward the surface in a kiss. The film cuts to more underwater traveling shots of undulating plants. A near-invisible dissolve allows old Iris to enter the watery frame, her appearance also accompanied by cymbals, though this time their celebration is muted. Like young

---

The DVD special features all revolve around the film's depiction of Alzheimer's and the Alzheimer's Association's wholehearted support, some would say appropriation, of the film: there is a filmed award ceremony in which the association honors the film, and a chilling plea from its spokesperson, David Hyde Pierce, that appeals to its American audience with a bottom-line argument: "the disease costs our country over a hundred billion dollars a year and without a research breakthrough the Alzheimer's epidemic alone will cost enough to bankrupt Medicare." Iris Murdoch the philosopher, the novelist, the teacher, has become a fundraising vehicle.

14. The match on action is "a continuity cut which splices two different views of the same action together at the same moment in the movement, making it seem to continue uninterrupted" (Bordwell and Thompson 480).

Iris, old Iris wears an expression of obvious pleasure. Old John joins old Iris, who smiles and says a few words, which are transformed into bubbles. John answers her with a similarly garbled remark. They join hands and move away from the camera up toward the water's surface. In this brief introductory sequence the watery space provides the opportunity for the softening of boundaries, both literally in the nearly invisible dissolves between shots, and figuratively in the suggestive cohabitation of various selves. The suggestion of continuity provided by the parallel experiences and actions of the two couples swimming separately and then together provides a template for much of the film. The fluidity of the scene, both literal and figurative, dissolves illusions of fixity, suggestively representing the slipperiness of aging, of time.

Later editorial incorporations of multiple temporalities in a single visual space allow for even more poignant doublings of continuity and change. Eyeline matches allow for double vision in which John sees Iris, and she returns his gaze as both young and old, a further cohabitation of the tenses that at once stresses continuity and makes plain the painful changes of age. In its simultaneous depiction of young and old, such editing expresses narrative identity and evokes the uncanniness of an older subject so constant and familiar, and yet so distressingly altered and strange.[15] However, the implications for time and aging in *Iris* remain problematic. The disruption of temporal categories can function at once as consolation and as a disturbing reminder of time's transformative effects. Though I read the editorial combination of tenses as a stripping away of the reductive illusion of age segmentation, the overemphasis on *similarity* between different selves risks a denial of difference. Certainly maintaining connections between "different but not incomparable selves" is difficult, particularly, one might add, when those selves are the time-altered version of a single person, and the desire to slip into totalizing models of sameness and difference may be tempting. *Iris* seems to oscillate between such categories, achieving brief moments of suspension that expose uncanny identity. The emphasis on temporal cohabitation threatens to reify identity-consistency over time, evoking models of core selfhood that strengthen the romantic pathos of Iris and John's eternal love.[16] But I believe the consolatory potential of

15. This cohabitation is a far cry from the distinct categories and narratives maintained in *The Notebook*. In *Iris* there is an obvious attempt to create visual similarities between the older and younger actors, whereas Gena Rowlands and Rachel McAdams of *The Notebook* bear no resemblance to one another; indeed it might take viewers some time to realize that they are both playing the same character.

16. Such a reading is reinforced by the snippets of old Iris lecturing on love and

sameness is undercut by the undeniability of change, which can make strict segmentation so appealing in the first place. The revelation of continuity, of some sameness, destroys what might be a more palatable illusion: that these two (younger and older Iris) are indeed entirely different people. In *Iris* the visualization of temporal continuity (as opposed to a discrete past and present) is what makes (pathological) old age so disturbing. In *The Notebook*, narrative connects past and present, functioning simultaneously as bridge and border that prevents infiltration, allowing minimal contact between distinct temporal selves. *Iris* perforates such a boundary, enabling temporal incursions that complicate the segmentation of age identities.

The film's biographical claims further complicate a reading of age and identity. *Iris* raises important questions regarding the telling of other person's stories, ethical concerns that I take up in the following discussion of fiction by Alice Munro and Jonathan Franzen. As with all biographies of deceased subjects, the telling of other people's stories places the biographer in a position of ethical responsibility.[17] Iris Murdoch's husband, John Bayley, functions as both witness and speaker for his disabled wife, providing testimony that Murdoch can no longer provide. The endurance of the Iris-John bond is central to the film, and, perhaps inevitably, it is as much John Bayley's story as it is Iris Murdoch's. The circumstances of Alzheimer's inhibit self-representation, and as a result the audience is given Murdoch *through* Bayley: the camera most often shares his point of view as an observer of Iris. Or, one could say, "It is Murdoch's story. But we have to let Bayley tell it." However, moments of continuity in the film infringe on the absolute alterity of dementia, preventing Murdoch from becoming a pathological object.

Though *Iris* relies on sentiment and nostalgia, often conveyed through romantic clichés, it maintains a complexity and obscurity absent from *The Notebook*, a film that concludes with an image of union, the simultaneous peaceful deaths of the long-devoted husband and wife. *Iris* concludes with images of solitude. In the end, the camera remains omniscient, the

---

goodness, which are intercut with images suggesting the early stages of her Alzheimer's. It is notable that this lecture is one of the only moments in which viewers see and hear a lucid old Iris. Accordingly, love appears as the only consistent aspect of Iris, the lecture forming a bridge between healthy youth and afflicted old age. Love, *Iris* suggests, is not dependent on language alone, and can persist even as speech and memory fade away.

17. As Anthony Kerby explains, "[t]elling a person's story tends invariably to plot the type of moral agent he or she is or was" (56). As well, biography demands a degree of legibility and coherence; biographers must "find shape and meaning within the apparently random circumstances of a life" (Holmes 16–17). Certainly a condition such as dementia complicates and reinforces such demands.

responsibility of witnessing transferred from John to the audience. The final image of Iris before her death shows her, alone in the hallway of the nursing home, dancing in the sunlight that streams through the many windows. In this final scene the camera feigns invisibility and old Iris appears unmediated and unprotected by her husband, making spectators the only witnesses to this private, impenetrable moment. This attention to nonlinguistic expression continues into the following scenes, in which we see John sadly sorting through his wife's clothes. The bright light of the previous scene is gone and the image is once again muted and dusty. The dimming effect of the disease has been visually transferred to John, who is caught in a shadowy grief. Alone, distraught, he now bears the burden of his wife's dementia; in the end it is John's suffering we witness. As John hugs her slip to his face, a rack focus—a shift in focus from one plane to another—brings the viewer's attention to a collection of stones, leaves, and dried algae on his wife's pillow. A stone slips off the pillow, and a match on action allows the stone to fall from the pillow into what one assumes is the same river that opened the film. The stone replaces the vibrant, swimming Iris of the film's opening, its lonely descent reflecting the final isolation enacted by late-life dementia. After Iris's death there can be no more collaboration, and her caregiver, her collaborator, her witness, is left stranded. The final scene enacts the transferal of ethical responsibility: viewers are now the only witnesses, left with a wordless visual image. The stone suggests incomprehensibility, otherness, and a degree of narrative opacity that denies straightforward teleology and closure. Resting on the riverbed the stone is still, but easily set into motion by an animal, a rough wind, a swimmer. This final emphasis on the material, the unpredictable, the distinctly inhuman, encourages viewers to consider the ending as partial. The stone's steadfast presence in contrast to Iris's absence once again points to the intermingling of continuity and constant change that is the foundation of narrative identity.

COLLABORATION AND CARE
Munro's Stories and *The Corrections*

Alice Munro, the prolific short story writer now in her seventies, has a writing career spanning five decades. Her early works, particularly the connected short story collections *The Lives of Girls and Women* (1971) and *Who Do You Think You Are?* (1978), have garnered much critical attention as feminist explorations of identity that provocatively explore the politics of gender and art. Critics have stressed her commitment to the everyday lives of women, her unflinching investigations into the by turns suffocating and satisfying world of the domestic. These early stories often engage with the tradition of the *Bildungsroman,* dramatizing the difficulties female characters encounter in aspiring to such a masculine model of growth and mature independence.[18] But Munro has also often turned her attention to older subjects, producing stories (particularly in her recent collections) that follow characters through maturity, into middle age and later life. Yet critical attention continues to rest on Munro's treatment of youth and young adulthood despite her recent attention to aging.[19]

Many of Munro's recent stories, such as "Powers," "Silence," and "The Bear Came Over the Mountain," focus on characters confronting the changes of aging into old age. In Munro's 2001 short story "The Bear Came Over the Mountain" (*Hateship*), recently made popular by Sarah Polley's film adaptation, *Away From Her,*[20] the onset of dementia disrupts the relationship of an older couple, Fiona and Grant. Fiona is institutionalized near the beginning of the story, and her subjectivity remains unavailable as the narrative oscillates between present and past, between Grant's struggle to comprehend Fiona's altered identity and his ignorance of her experience of their shared past. Through these temporal shifts the reader learns that Grant is a retired professor of Anglo-Saxon and Nordic literature, that he had several rather tempestuous affairs with students, and that the couple lived in Fiona's parents' house, where they led intellectual, reclusive lives. Readers learn little of Fiona herself in the depictions of the past, which are mostly focalized through Grant. Grant's knowledge of his wife is significantly limited; he has tended to think of Fiona as delightfully foreign, as a dynamic but mysterious being. The scenes from the past expose how Grant has relied on Fiona's persistent otherness to justify his

18. This is particularly the case in *Lives of Girls and Women,* in which the protagonist Del observes and eventually encounters the trying, often self-negating demands of womanhood. This collection has proved to be a critical favorite, continuing to appear on many university syllabi.

19. For example, a search of the Modern Language Association database produces twenty-five citations on *Lives of Girls and Women* and eleven dealing with childhood, whereas only two sources appear to deal explicitly with aging, old age, or maturity in Munro's work.

20. Polley's film is interesting for its rearrangement of the story's ethical potential. By muting Grant's sexism and objectification of women, which are so clearly displayed in Munro's story, the film consigns much of the ambiguity and moral conflict to the background. The film is a powerful love story, but many of the insights into identity, which are so important to the story, are absent.

betrayals, regarding her as a delightfully opaque object, denying her sub-jectivity in order to indulge his own transgressive desires. Grant discards any possibility of obligation to this other, but Fiona's dementia forces a new engagement with responsibility.

According to Naomi Morgenstern, revelations of responsibility are characteristic of Munro's stories, which frequently "address the question of why it is that the ethical insight—that the other exists beyond the self—needs to be repeated" (72). But this ethical insight raises a number of problems, as Morgenstern makes clear in a series of questions: "How can one reach out to the other without doing violence to their otherness in the very attempt to fold them into the self's understanding? How can an encounter with alterity not do violence to the encountering subject . . . ?" (71). Munro's stories repeatedly depict characters teetering along such an ethical high wire, often exposing the impossibility of maintaining such a balancing act. Morgenstern deftly elucidates the ethical import of various Munro stories, in particular, how distinctly gendered ethical dilemmas encourage a reconsideration of "femininity" (73). Stories such as "Post and Beam," "Meneseteung," and "My Mother's Dream" involve female protagonists encountering a critical but largely impossible responsibility for other women. In "Bear," the ethical crisis is no longer one experienced between two women, but rather involves a husband responding to his dementia-afflicted wife, an unexpected call to awareness and responsibility at odds with the husband's history of carelessness and infidelity. Grant's is a past lacking any evidence of ethical insight or empathetic response. It is only Fiona's dementia, which exaggerates unfamiliarity to a staggering degree, that forces Grant to finally confront alterity, both the otherness of other people and the otherness of self.

Fiona's dementia asserts itself in a great disordering—of linear chronology, of linguistic codes, of navigational cues. Dementia caused by Alzheimer's disease involves a selective deterioration of the brain that allows for some recognizable consistency of identity in the midst of alarming strangeness. The selectivity of dementia can actually inhibit a caregiver's efforts to come to terms with the alterations of the disease, as moments of familiarity, the sudden appearance of an identity assumed lost, can undermine any attempts to adjust to the strange newness of the condition. In Munro's story, Fiona's familiarity causes Grant to doubt their choice to move her into a care facility. As she prepares to leave the house, Grant reflects that, at age seventy and suffering from dementia, she is remarkably unchanged: "*She looked just like herself on this day*" (276, original emphasis). The grammar of Grant's rumination is telling; he produces an analogy that compares the thing, in this case, Fiona, to itself, producing a closed circuit of comparison that is impossible to contradict. The circular relation between the two pronouns, "she," and "herself," reflects Fiona's inscrutability; with no outside basis for comparison she is, of course, always successfully "herself." This invulnerable model of identity assessment is key to Grant's perception of Fiona, and to the relationship that results from such perception. The inclusion of multiple incidents remembered from Grant's past attests to his ongoing assessment of Fiona as invariably and fetchingly opaque. The scene involving Fiona's move to Meadowlake follows directly after a description of their betrothal, in which Grant accepts Fiona's spontaneous proposal because "[h]e wanted never to be away from her. She had the spark of life" (275). Bewitched by her vitality, Grant accepts her subjectivity as entirely mysterious, often quaintly so.

His interpretation of Fiona, or more precisely his acceptance of her very *un*interpretability, provokes Grant to perceive her early signs of dementia, what the medical community term "mild cognitive impairments," as signs of her enduring eccentricity. When Grant notices a proliferation of yellow notes stuck on cupboards and drawers, he sees an extension of her "mystifying and touching" tendency to write all sorts of things down, from book titles and errands to her domestic schedule (276). In fact, as Grant quickly learns, the yellow notes are Fiona's effort to attach signs to their referents; to forestall the disintegration of all connections between words and the everyday world around her, she must literally paste words onto objects. The labeling triggers Grant to recall "a story about the German soldiers on border patrol in Czechoslovakia during the war. Some Czech had told him that each of the patrol dogs wore a sign that said *Hund*. Why? Said the Czechs, and the Germans said, Because that is a *hund*" (276). The story groups Fiona's pathological symptoms with quirky, *foreign* behavior, the bizarre traditions of strangers. Fiona has not so much *become* a stranger as been *revealed* as one, the exaggerated idiosyncratic actions distinguishing her as a foreigner.[21]

21. The story's attention to signification depicts language as a disorienting facade, one both imposed (the sticky notes must be attached to their referents; the *Hund* must literally wear his linguistic identity) and indisputable; the circle of signification reveals that the *Hund* is a *Hund* and Fiona is herself. But the narrator insists she looked *like* herself, employing the language of seeming, and untrustworthy appearances. The language of deceit recurs throughout the story, and Coral Ann Howells points out the numerous mentions of "tricks" and "disguises" (*Contemporary* 58, 60). An attention to jokes and tricks recurs throughout Munro's fiction, a recurrence critics have associated with her larger preoccupation with the inadequacy and duplicity of language, her "fascination with the very limits of representation, especially in language" (Heble 4).

After an imposed three-month separation from Fiona, meant to allow her to adjust to her new environment, Grant experiences a new excitement as he prepares to visit Meadowlake: "He was full of solemn tingling, as in the old days on the morning of his first planned meeting with a new woman. . . . There was an expectation of discovery, almost a spiritual expansion. Also timidity, humility, alarm" (287). Fiona has been transformed into the "other woman," other than his wife, other than herself. The situation provokes a novel gesture: Grant buys her flowers, though "[h]e had never presented flowers to Fiona before. Or to anyone else" (287). Grant himself becomes altered by Fiona's condition, a diffusion of difference that triggers self-consciousness and alienation. He experiences himself as a character "in a cartoon" (287), engaging in emotions and behavior other than his own. Upon arrival at Meadowlake, he finds Fiona distinctly familiar yet strange: "He could not throw his arms around her. Something about her voice and smile, familiar as they were, something about the way she seemed to be guarding the players and even the coffee woman from him—as well as him from their displeasure—made that not possible" (289). The reference to Fiona's protective air suggests a community unavailable to Grant, an exclusion that becomes increasingly obvious as the story continues. In typical Munro fashion there is a reversal that finds Grant occupying the role of stranger as a result of Fiona's disease; in recognizing her otherness Grant comes to glimpse his own strangeness. This insight has great ethical potential if the witness can move toward the kind of difficult, respectful response that Morgenstern elaborates, but there is also risk involved as the witness's selfhood is strained by increased awareness of his or her own instability, an awakening to the universal strangeness described in Kristeva's *Strangers to Ourselves,* her assertion that otherness lurks within every subject. No longer permitted opportunities to participate in Fiona's life, Grant is confined to the position of

---

Often Munro's stories disrupt the transparency of language, calling into question the very act of representation. As a result her stories often prompt a degree of self-reflexivity in their readers that makes us aware of our own role as witnesses. As Magdalene Redekop explains, "The pleasure of reading Alice Munro is, in the final analysis, that we catch ourselves in the act of looking" (3). This positioning of readers as self-conscious witnesses raises further questions regarding ethical insight, as readers become increasingly aware of the "otherness of others" and the responsibility such awareness entails. One quickly realizes that any desires to determine true identities, motives, and allegiances are in vain, inevitably frustrated by a narrative of reversals and tricks. This narrative and linguistic precariousness complements the problems of identity and understanding that the story dramatizes. This is a story of the *un*canny as a term of reversal, of *un*raveling, of *un*steadying, *un*settling.

observer, and he spends much of his time at Meadowlake tagging along with his wife, a tolerated "nuisance" (291). Understandably, this enforced role of outsider seriously alters his relationship with his wife and arguably introduces Grant to a new ethical awareness. Dementia brings alterity to the fore, and Grant is forced to confront a mysteriousness that is no longer quaint and far from comforting.

In the past Fiona had been a useful other, one that reinforced Grant's own selfhood. The disappearance of this stabilizing, benign other whose subjectivity Grant could easily efface now disrupts Grant's own selfhood. When Kristy, a staff member at Meadowlake, asks him whether he is "glad to see her participating and everything," Grant cannot respond directly, but rather answers with reference to himself: "Does she even know who I am?" (290). In a sense, Grant's question is a predictable response to Kristy, since he is accustomed to locating himself via Fiona. Much of what follows in the story involves Grant's difficult observations of Fiona outside of any relation to himself. Unable to recognize Grant as her husband, Fiona continues to exist as Fiona, as other, forcing Grant to glimpse his own insignificance. Early in the story, Grant dreams of one of his previous infidelities, a dream that provides readers with some sense of his perception of Fiona and their past relationship. In the dream Grant receives an accusatory letter from the roommate of one of his student lovers: "Its style was sanctimonious and hostile, threatening in a whining way—he put the writer down as a latent lesbian. The girl herself was someone he had parted from decently, and it seemed unlikely that she would want to make a fuss, let alone try to kill herself, which was what the letter was apparently, elaborately, trying to tell him" (283). As the dream continues Grant finds himself in a lecture hall filled with "cold-eyed young women in black robes" who sit in the "last, highest row" and "never [take] their bitter stares off him" (284). Fiona appears in the lecture hall as well, her expression and positioning ("in the first row") a direct contrast to the "flock" of menacing women. Her response to the threatening letter is dismissive: "Oh, phooey. . . . Girls that age are always going around talking about how they'll kill themselves," a reaction that, though supportive, seems flimsy and unaware of the "black ring [that] was thickening, drawing in, all around his windpipe, all around the top of the room" (284). In this dream, Fiona's comments express the version of identity Grant has constructed for her; she is supportive and strange, removed from the shifting public morals and opinions that are encircling him.

Fiona's condition initiates an ironic reversal; as reluctant witness Grant comes to occupy the territory he had always reserved for others, in particular for women, whom he has typically desired for their intoxicating, bewildering strangeness. Meadowlake's ability to redefine normality thrusts Grant into exile, as he can witness Fiona and her friends only from a distance. But normality depends on a majority's ability to exclude others, and an influx of the young and able-bodied on Meadowlake's visiting day reverses the ordinariness of the institutionalized: "And now surrounded by a variety of outsiders these insiders did not look like such regular people after all. Female chins might have had their bristles shaved to the roots and bad eyes might be hidden by patches or dark lenses, inappropriate utterances might be controlled by medication, but some glaze remained, a haunted rigidity—as if people were content to become memories of themselves, final photographs" (296). Visitors dissolve the community and normality of the "insiders" by dragging along with them the restrictive expectations that disallow the institutionalized to betray their altered state. Newness, strangeness, must be contained and hidden, resulting in haunted subjects, people fixed by the oppressive weight of the past. The passage includes the language of traces, of unsettling remainders that infiltrate the reassuring facades. The references to haunting, memories, and photographs speak to the permeation of tenses, the failure of attempts to segment and isolate past and present selves. Despite efforts to impose fixity and conceal the effects of temporal identity, "some glaze remained." The introduction of "outsiders" into the institution enforces a youth-based version of normality that dissolves the ordinariness of the insiders' new, "perverse" selves that leave unsettling traces on the performed selves manufactured for the visitors' benefit. As a result, these alterations of time haunt the imposed identity of a remembered self. The "insiders" become memories, photographs, fixed signs of themselves, simulacra that recall the early description of Fiona as looking "just like herself." In effect, the debilitations of old age transform subjects into imitations of themselves, often highly accurate copies, but copies nonetheless. Thus, the not-yet-old, or more specifically, the not-yet-afflicted-by-age, deny the otherness of human temporality by refusing to accept the cohabitation of continuity and change. By opting for one or the other, they deny the more unsettling possibility of uncanny aging, of subjects, of selves, at once the same and different, familiar and strange. In forcing the Meadowlake residents to function as memories and photographs, their visitors deny the otherness of the other.

As a result of his long periods of observation, Grant comes to occupy a kind of liminal space, removed from both sides of the visitor-resident divide. He is privy to various performances in his role as witness, and this alternate position facilitates a new ethical awareness in Grant. An ambiguously focalized passage describing the lives of the Meadowlake residents depicts such new insight:

> People here—even the ones who did not participate in any activities but sat around watching the doors or looking out the windows—were living a busy life in their heads (not to mention the life of their bodies, the portentous shifts in their bowels, the stabs and twinges everywhere along the line), and that was a life that in most cases could not very well be described or alluded to in front of visitors. All they could do was wheel or somehow propel themselves and hope to come up with something that could be displayed or talked about. (297)

Here the reader can glimpse the disconcerting abjection of old age. If one does indeed detect something of Grant's perspective here, then it is a perspective in transformation, showing an emerging willingness to acknowledge the incomprehensible, but nonetheless existent, subjectivity of others.

At Meadowlake, Fiona forms a close bond with another resident, Aubrey, an intimacy that excludes her husband. Grant continues to visit his wife, but remains somewhat of an outsider; Fiona treats him "as some persistent visitor who took a special interest in her. Or perhaps even as a nuisance who must be prevented, according to her old rules of courtesy, from realizing that he was one" (291–92). So committed is Fiona to this new relationship that when Aubrey is taken home by his own wife, she becomes despondent, eating little, barely moving, only "weeping weakly, on a bench by the wall" (306). In an effort to save Fiona from being moved to the second floor where she can get long-term bedcare, a floor reserved for "the people who . . . had really lost it" (298), Grant makes a visit to Aubrey and his wife, Marian, asking that Aubrey be allowed to return to Meadowlake, if only as a visitor. After some subtle negotiations and an implied offer of companionship, Aubrey is allowed to return. But Fiona's allegiances have shifted once more and she rejects Aubrey as a stranger, rejoicing instead at Grant's return:

> "I'm happy to see you," she said, and pulled his earlobes.
> "You could have just driven away," she said. "Just driven away without a care in the world and forsook me. Forsooken me. Forsaken."
> He kept his face against her white hair, her pink scalp, her sweetly shaped skull. He said, Not a chance. (322)

Even this scene of possible reconciliation bears the traces of unsettling strangeness. Though Fiona expresses a familiarity through her ambiguous manipulation of language, Grant is aware of unmistakable alteration, which his focalization associates with decay: "Her skin or her breath gave off a faint new smell, a smell that seemed to him like that of the stems of cut flowers left too long in their water" (321). The unpleasant *new* odor of decomposition coexists with the pleasant familiarity of her "sweetly shaped skull" (322). Though she "retrieve[s], with an effort, some bantering grace" (322), her embrace alerts Grant to the undeniable changes of age. These final lines remain highly enigmatic, as Coral Ann Howells makes clear in her analysis of the collection as a whole. She regards Grant's "Not a chance" as "an echo of his old duplicitous reassurances," emphasizing the "indeterminancy" of the closing scene (77). She sees this indeterminacy as part of the larger "promise of unpredictability" at work in the collection as a whole, which exposes the difficulty in distinguishing reality from simulacrum (77). But while Howells sees the mysteriousness of liminal spaces between the real and the imagined, I see an obscurity in this story more directly related to the inscrutability of temporality and identity. It is certainly the case that Grant's sincerity is indeterminable, that it is impossible to know whether the scene is indeed a "real encounter between husband and wife," whether there is "genuine emotional warmth on Fiona's part or just in Grant's imagination" (77). But I believe there is a larger, and perhaps more frightening, indeterminacy at work here.

In "Bear," later life compels a rereading of life stories that exposes the flexibility of interpretation, and consequently, of identity. Fiona's dementia demands not only rereading, but also a readjustment of expectations and allegiances, a new engagement with ethical responsibility. The process of aging into old age, complicated by Fiona's dementia, introduces Grant to a new awareness of responsibility that moves him to moments of ethical empathy in which he glimpses both his own strangeness, and the familiarity of the other. Between absolute alterity and the violent containment of the "other's otherness with an economy of the same" (Morgenstern 72), diacritical hermeneutics depends on a fragile balancing of respect and recognition that introduces us to our own uncanniness, an acknowledgment of "ourselves-as-others." Fiona's dementia introduces Grant to a new model of relating that provides the potential for ethical witnessing and interpretation, for empathy and the appreciation of another's needs. Excluded from participation, Grant is forced to assume a role he has refused throughout his life, that of the witness whose primary job is to listen and observe. This new position of witness leads Grant toward ethical insight, toward a recognition of and respect for Fiona's otherness that prompts an uncharacteristic act of selflessness—the return of Aubrey to Meadowlake—in which he puts the other's needs before his own.

Some of Munro's earlier work also shows a preoccupation with ethical crises prompted by aging, particularly aging into old age complicated by illness. *Who Do You Think You Are?* is a collection of connected short stories that follow protagonist Rose through her childhood in a small, poor town; her subsequent move to a nearby city; her lucrative but unhappy marriage to the son of a wealthy department store baron; and her subsequent divorce. The two final stories depict Rose in her maturity returning to sites of her youth. In particular, the story "Spelling" concerns Rose in her middle age (her marriage is over; her children are grown; her career is established, if not always flourishing) and her new responsibility for her aged and ailing stepmother, Flo. When Rose returns to her childhood home she realizes the severity of Flo's disability: the house is jumbled and dirty and Flo has difficulty recognizing Rose as her stepdaughter. As well, Flo has developed some bizarre habits (the table is always set; she drinks maple syrup from the bottle). Rose's self-serving fantasies of devoted caregiving quickly dissolve as Flo's strangeness triggers the recollection of past narratives of frustration and disappointment, revealing Flo's difficult behavior in old age as a disturbing evolution of her past transgressions. Flo in the present is often obstinate and demanding to a pathological degree; Flo in the past was willful, stubborn, and racist. As with Fiona, the afflicted other in "Bear," Flo's delusional old age modifies a longstanding strangeness. These stories suggest dementia as a pathological amplification of pre-existing otherness, an exaggeration that forces loved ones to acknowledge such otherness and adapt to its demands. In these two stories, much of the pathos of dementia comes from the flashes of connection and understanding that seem to momentarily dispel dementia's murky incomprehensibility. The stories represent distressing, even frightful alterity; but they also depict the potential for a kind of pleasurable collaboration. Dementia makes such moments entirely unpredictable, but their existence thwarts the urge to consign the afflicted person to the realm of the monstrous other. Familiarity can return suddenly, forcefully, when one least expects it, an uncanny return of selfhood where the unafflicted were tempted to assume none existed any longer.

Rose first confronts the problem of responding to seemingly absolute otherness when she visits the County Home in preparation for Flo's institutionalization. There she meets a woman whom age has transformed into a kind of automated object, an encounter that leads to a revelation similar to that experienced by Grant in "Bear," a budding awe at the incomprehensible, yet undeniable, personhood of those suffering the severe debilitations of old age and illness: "Taking in oxygen, giving out carbon dioxide, they continued to participate in the life of the world" ("Spelling" 226–27). Rose's visit to the County Home forces her to consider the otherness of persons seriously debilitated by aging, those who are unable to participate in the everyday world of language and movement. She confronts head-on the limits of her understanding and imagination and the difficulty of responding ethically to a radically altered subjectivity. The story's title refers to the only verbal communication still available to the woman Rose meets at the County Home, a communication that becomes an "expression of her humanity" (Redekop 140). "Crouched in her crib, diapered, dark as a nut, with three tufts of hair," the nameless old woman the nurse calls "Aunty" will spell out any word she hears (Munro 227). Infantilized and abject, "the old woman" continues to exist, to "participate in the life of the world," though hers is an incomprehensible existence spent "meandering through that emptiness or confusion that nobody on this side can do more than guess at" (228). Rose tries to imagine such an unusual relationship with language, how words might have a kind of foreign vitality to them, making each one seem "alive as a new animal," coming together to form "[a] parade of private visitors" (228). But this is only one of a list of possible subjectivities Rose imagines. Once again, Munro's fiction suggests that language is not a simple container for meaning, but a demonstration of the impossibility of pure communication, what Heble identifies as Munro's "fascination with the very limits of representation" (4). Words signify in very different ways for the various speakers and listeners, writers and readers. Language in "Spelling" is transformed from a transparent medium to an opaque material; it no longer contains meaning, but exists on its own terms, without reference to linguistic structures of meaning. The story's title—"Spelling"—points to the central importance of the scene and its exploration of the difficulties involved in interpreting personhood and subjectivity, the tendency to associate identity with vivacious youth. Rose's witnessing of the spelling woman initiates an insight into otherness that makes possible a new kind of respect and communication that will reappear in the story's concluding scene.

The majority of the story shows Rose and Flo at odds, with very little suggestion of understanding or collaboration between the two women. They appear distant, almost strangers, each vaguely ashamed of the other. The story's final pages involve a sequence of scenes depicting numerous failures of communication between Rose and Flo, but culminating in a scene in which the difficulties and demands of aging make possible a new kind of understanding, one able to incorporate miscommunication. The earlier depictions of frustrated communication show the two women at loggerheads, each cocooned in her own resentful superiority. In one episode the appearance of Rose's bared breast in a televised theatre performance inspires Flo to write a letter of admonishment. The letter does the opposite of communicating, becoming instead a testament to the pair's inability to comprehend one another. Far from bridging the gap between them, the letter draws attention to its expanse, giving Rose a "fresh and overwhelming realization" of that "gulf" (231). Flo's letter becomes a kind of party trick for Rose, who reads it aloud to her friends "for comic effect," a betrayal that transforms a supposed intimate—Rose's stepmother—into a figure of public mockery (230). Here the comedy works in only one direction: Flo is the unaware, and one would assume unwilling, butt of the joke, while Rose relishes the humor. This is not comedic collaboration. Flo's sincere admonishment is so bewildering to Rose that it can be understood only as absurdity, the nonsensically outdated prudishness of an old woman from a small town: "These reproaches of Flo's made as much sense as a protest about raising umbrellas, a warning against eating raisins" (231). This narrative of Flo's indignation is followed by one in which the shaming is reversed, with Flo committing the humiliating offense. When Rose invites Flo to an award reception where she will be honored, Flo's racist language exposes her small-town naïveté. "Look at the Nigger!" Flo cries upon glimpsing another award recipient (231): "Her tone was one of simple, gratified astonishment, as if she had been peering down the Grand Canyon or seen oranges growing on a tree" (231–32). The similes construct Flo's outburst as a reaction to something strange and remarkable, and it is this very reaction that ironically exposes Flo herself as exactly that. To the other ceremony attendees, the "bearded and beaded, the unisexual and the unashamedly un-Anglo-Saxon" (232), Flo is something strange, though perhaps more repellent than remarkable.

It is only within the altered circumstances of aging and dementia that the possibility of collaboration and understanding arises as Rose gains new ethical insight, as suggested in her reaction to the old spelling woman. The story's final scene demonstrates how a new communicative potential grows out of a shared appreciation of absurdity. It is Munro's characteristic use of humor that most powerfully confirms the prevailing humanity of the delusional other, providing both characters and readers with a glimpse of a largely incomprehensible, but undeniable, subjectivity that frustrates the simple objectification of difference. When Rose brings one of Flo's old wigs to the County Home where Flo now lives, Flo mistakes the wig for a dead gray squirrel. Rose explains that the hairy thing is, in fact, a wig and the two begin to laugh. Rose looks at the wig and considers that it "did look like a dead cat or squirrel, even though she had washed and brushed it; it was a disturbing-looking object." Flo exclaims, "I thought what is she doing bringing me a dead squirrel! If I put it on somebody'd be sure to take a shot at me." Rose responds by sticking it on her own head to "continue the comedy, and Flo laughed so that she rocked back and forth in her crib" (232). The episode depicts a shared pleasure in slapstick, portraying the communicative potential of the absurd. Rose not only humors Flo's delusions by behaving according to the peculiar expectations of dementia but also delights her with a comedic display that facilitates a shared pleasure previously unavailable to stepmother and stepdaughter. Rose and Flo enjoy a moment of comical absurdity, finding some respite, even comfort, in shared silliness. Rose's increasing openness to the incomprehensibility of the other produces a new experience of *collaborative* humor distinctly kinder than her previous mocking comedy. The unexpected joke suggests that an ethical response may come as the result of an overturning of rational meaning. Understanding transpires in moments of nonsense and absurdity, such as "Aunty's" spelling or Rose's slapstick. These moments involve an alternative form of dialogue, one that maintains a productive space between self and other; the "gulf" between Rose and Flo remains, but they can hear one another's cries from the other side. In "Spelling," the alterations of aging compel Rose's consideration of otherness, an otherness she eventually struggles to acknowledge and even respect.

The moment of comedy is quickly followed by Flo's delusional references to her gallstones and dead husband:

> When she got her breath Flo said, "What am I doing with these damn sides up on my bed? Are you and Brian behaving yourselves? Don't fight, it gets on your father's nerves. Do you know how many gallstones they took out of me? Fifteen! One as big as a pullet's egg. I got them somewhere. I'm going to take them home." She pulled at the sheets, searching. "They were in a bottle."
>
> "I've got them already," said Rose. "I took them home."
>
> "Did you? Did you show your father?"
>
> "Yes."
>
> "Oh, well, that's where they are then," said Flo, and she lay down and closed her eyes.

The story ends here. Her misunderstanding is not mocked or corrected or even interpreted by Rose. The omniscient narrator's remarks are descriptive rather than interpretive: "She pulled at the sheets, searching. . . . [S]he lay down and closed her eyes." There is no indication that Rose directs the narration; instead, readers are given only her verbalized responses to Flo. By concluding with Flo's language and movements the story privileges incomprehensibility, depicting otherness without a narrator's interpretation or explanation. Not only has Rose taken on the role of witness, willing to listen to uninterpretable testimony, but readers are similarly pulled toward Flo, fashioned by the narration into witnesses to what Felman calls the "scandal of illness," to the trauma of afflicted old age (4). Here one sees ethical responsibility in action, a respect for otherness that causes Rose to participate in, rather than "correct," absurdity. It is here, in the uninterpreted language of delusion, that readers glimpse the positive potential of empathetic witnessing, a dialogic model of relations in which understanding and misunderstanding can coexist.

This kind of paradoxical relationship, with its moments of fruitful, and even pleasurable, miscommunication, is far from the alienation and horror of later-life dementia experienced in Jonathan Franzen's *The Corrections*. In Franzen's novel, Alfred, the aging Lambert family patriarch, undergoes a painfully isolated descent into delusions induced by Parkinson's disease. The fleeting insights into otherness that facilitate moments of responsibility and exchange in "Bear" and "Spelling" give way to the terrifyingly absolute alienation in *The Corrections*. In Franzen's novel, narrative perspective is dispersed among the various family members, allowing the reader to consider events from a variety of angles. But the varied focalization is countered by a paucity of communication between the family members. To a large degree, these characters are strangers to one another, and there are a number of references to their fear of one another and their trepidation at the prospect of forced interaction. At the head of this detached family is Alfred, whose preference for guarded existence is largely responsible for the family's estrangement. Alfred aligns seclusion with personhood ("Without privacy there was no point in being an individual" [465]) and separation with love ("The odd truth about Alfred was that love, for him, was a matter not of approaching but of keeping away" [526]). As a result, the novel depicts five characters, parents Alfred and Enid and their three children, Gary, Chip, and Denise, trapped in often desperate, and overwhelmingly private, struggles against the unhappiness of their lives. This ethos of exclusionary identity has serious repercussions as the characters, particularly Alfred, age. For Alfred, the process of aging into old age is complicated by the debilitations of Parkinson's disease; body trem-ors, hallucinations, and memory failure flout his demand for authorita-tive independence. For Alfred, the unavoidable consequence of an old age complicated by illness is a crushing loss of self. In ascribing to a masculine model of rigid, authority-based identity, Alfred inhibits the possibility of the ethical insight experienced in Munro's stories. Alfred experiences the uncanniness of pathological aging only as a horrifying unraveling of self that leaves him stranded as empowered independence gives way to terrify-ing alienation.[22] Alfred's later-life illness forces a debilitating confrontation with radical impermanence that is without the consolations of collabora-tion represented in the other texts. Unlike the victims of dementia in *Bar-ney's Version*, *Iris*, "Bear," and "Spelling," Alfred has no witness to hear his stories, no comedic collaborator.

Alfred's dementia manifests itself in terrifying, grotesque hallucina-tions in which the "filth" he has so vigorously rejected throughout his life returns to haunt him: a "turd" appears in the night to taunt him, screaming obscenities, dirtying the walls and bedding (284–87). These hallucinations reflect the frightening confusion that results from utter privacy, the strictly insular self-reliance of a closed man. Throughout his life he has refused others' attempts to listen and collaborate, the efforts of his wife and chil-dren to participate in his life narratives. As his illness worsens the stories he tells himself about his life get out of hand, his suffering aggravated by his devotion to a rigid model of selfhood that relies on impermeable barriers between self and other, perceiving others as dangerous opponents, duplici-tous strangers. As a result, the recognition of otherness within is absolutely terrifying. An identity based on unrelenting rigidity and restraint cannot tolerate the appearance of its own instability and uncanniness; these hallu-cinations tear his world to shreds, transforming him into a railing, desper-ate man. His otherness, his failure, must be hidden. As a result, there are few opportunities for collaboration and caregiving, or for ethical insight.

All that Alfred has rejected, in particular his own difference and desire, returns in his repulsive hallucination. It is notable that the phantom appears directly after the narration of an episode from the past in which

---

22. Franzen's personal essay "My Father's Brain," concerning his father's deteriora-tion due to Alzheimer's, reflects a similar bias for independence and mastery. In the essay Franzen mourns his father's agonizing loss of abilities but finds some solace in evidence of his father's enduring authority and force. For example, an unsent letter "become[s] an emblem of invisibly heroic exertions of the will" (*How to Be Alone* 34); his father's refusal of a swab to clear his mouth shows he was "determined to die and to die, as best he could, on his own terms" (36).

he had reluctantly indulged his sexual desires, what he regards as "a defilement in pursuit of satisfaction" (282). For Alfred, witnessing is linked to judgment, to castigation and shame. After his "defilement" of his wife he imagines his unborn daughter as a "witness to such harm. Witness to a tautly engorged little brain that dipped in and out. . . . Alfred lay catching his breath and repenting his defiling of the baby" (281). He sees sex as "the pleasure he'd stolen," the "stabbing she'd endured" (281). The hallucinated turd is a manifestation of the judgmental witness he fears, one who will expose his shameful failings. In Kristeva's terms, excrement is clearly abject, at once unavoidably human and utterly other. The abject exposes the fragility of the border between the "I" and "that which I am not," which is necessary for our constitution as subjects, the ease with which difference, and therefore meaning, can be collapsed. In other words, excrement, the abject, is "what I permanently thrust aside in order to live. These body fluids, this defilement, this shit are what life withstands, hardly and with difficulty, on the part of death" (Kristeva, *Powers* 3). According to Kristeva, a disavowal of shit represents an attempt to jettison the decay of the body, to refuse an underlying sameness that threatens to replace structures of meaning based on difference with a kind of grotesque continuity. Alfred's abject turd flouts his longing for order and control by destroying boundaries and abolishing difference. It is "sociopathic," "loose," "opposed to all strictures," promising to sully his clothes with a stinking trace of animality (Franzen 285). In this rather heavy-handed symbolism, Alfred's aging, his illness—conditions that the novel repeatedly intertwines—produce an utter loss of control that undoes the identity Alfred has worked so hard to preserve, a selfhood based on discipline and control.

"Civilization depends upon restraint," Alfred responds to the turd's championing of self-indulgence (285). The hallucination reflects a distinctly Freudian reading of civilization and identity, producing a nightmare vision of emancipation in which the hedonistic Id has entirely overcome the responsible Ego; otherness has invaded selfhood. This symbolic struggle between Alfred's devotion to his "civilized" facade and his own repressed desires participates in the discourse of uncanny age. Alfred's aging and debilitation produce an identity in conflict as the facades of authority and stability give way to a chaotic multiplicity. It is no coincidence that "[t]he turd had an attitude, a tone of voice, that Alfred found eerily familiar but couldn't quite place" (286). Alfred hallucinates a confrontation with a narrative of self he would seek to deny, a narrative of licentiousness, eager domination, and xenophobic rage. When Alfred exclaims that the hideous intruder belongs in jail, it responds with a page-long tirade that exposes the ugly underbelly of Alfred's exclusionary instincts. Alfred, the turd explains, would see "*everything* in jail" and it proceeds to list the many offending others, others whose apparent messiness necessitates punishment: kids "drop food on the carpet," Polynesians "track sand in the house, get fish juice on the furniture," "pubescent chickies" expose their "honkers," "Negroes" drink and sweat and dance and make noise, Caribbeans carry "viruses," the Chinese eat slimy food, women "trail Kleenexes and Tampaxes everywhere they go," and the list goes on (287). This tirade against the perceived excesses of others exposes Alfred's compulsive rejection of otherness as dangerous and vile, a violent refusal that reflects his terror at his own crumbling identity. Alfred anxiously projects frightening, repulsive otherness onto women, children, and visible minorities in response to his growing awareness of his own undeniable and offensive otherness.

Toward the end of the novel, when the family has come together for what promises to be their final reunion, the severity of Alfred's illness becomes undeniable. As the three children observe the painful effects of the disease, they have various opportunities to provide their father with care. Gary, Denise, and Chip assist their father despite their own unease, even disgust, at the changes of age. They witness their father in abject vulnerability—struggling to bathe, dress, give himself an enema. Invariably the children adopt, if only briefly, the role of caregiver, a function they find painful and disorienting. Alfred's pathological aging introduces his children to a kind of horror that shakes their own selfhood. When Gary walks in on Alfred standing naked in the bathtub, hallucinating, he finds his father's uncanniness disturbingly contagious:

> Gary himself was infected, there in the middle of the night, by his father's disease. As the two of them collaborated on the problem of the diaper, . . . Gary, too, had a sensation of things dissolving around him, of a night that consisted of creepings and shiftings and metamorphoses. He had the sense that there were many more than two people in the house beyond the bedroom door . . . phantoms. (501)

This is the dark side of aging's radical instability. Here, collaboration results in a mutual haunting that upsets any sense of reliable stability and drives apart rather than draws together the collaborating agents. Gary's insights expose him to a recognition of otherness that disturbs the foundations of his own subjectivity. The world around Gary seems to be in the process of disintegrating, the unified singularity of identity an impossible fiction: there are no longer only "two people in the house beyond the bedroom door"—the world has begun a process of multiplication that destabilizes meaning and identity. The inclusion of the term "metamorphoses" is integral; Gary is unwillingly taking on the uncanny vision of radical impermanence. Gary himself becomes afflicted, in Felman's terms, as "an unwitting, inadvertent . . . *involuntary witness*" to "an illness whose effects explode any capacity for explanation or rationalization" (Felman and Lamb 4, original emphasis). He becomes witness to the radical alterity of temporality that appears as aging into old age.

Throughout his life Alfred has no witnesses or collaborators. There is little possibility of collaboration, exchange, or sharing because these are not part of his aggressively independent vocabulary. He interprets his sudden need for assistance as pathetic, as a failure. His children's assistance comes without his request or appreciation. It is only near the novel's end, when Alfred is overwhelmed by despair at his helplessness, that he calls out for help. However, his final call to the other, a call for annihilation, is in vain. He would prefer nonbeing to impotent existence and asks his son to relieve him from the suffering of helplessness. But his request is one of total self-interest, one that can be made only by ignoring the humanity of the other. Despite the fact that such an act would do excessive violence to his son, Alfred's need for private independence trumps his concern for others. Indeed, his earlier decision *not* to commit suicide was the result of his suffocating need for privacy and control, the extreme exposure of his blasted body turning him away from death: "But to be seen as the finite carcass in a sea of blood and bone chips and gray matter—to inflict that version of himself on other people—was a violation of privacy so profound it seemed it would outlive him" (466). Though his justifications show an ostensible concern for others, his desire to protect others from trauma is also, or even primarily, a self-protective urge.

When Alfred is finally transferred to "Deepmire" care facility, Alfred regards himself as a prisoner of a brutal authority bent on revenge. His rage at his own helplessness continues to surface in violent racist outbursts, this time expressed as a hatred for the black staff. Old age, particularly pathological old age, devastates the power and privilege he has enjoyed all his life as a middle-class white man. His impotent dependence on others is not only embarrassing to him but also enraging, since he is now at the mercy of those he once dominated. Old age and illness have introduced him to the space of otherness, an otherness he resists by attempting to reinstate the boundaries and hierarchies that have always maintained his identity. Alfred transforms a black, female staff member at Deepmire into a demon bent on revenge: "The big black lady, the mean one, the bastard, was the one he had to keep an eye on. She intended to make his life a hell. She stood at the far end of the prison yard throwing him significant glances to remind him that she hadn't forgotten him, she was still in hot pursuit of her vendetta" (553). Alfred's delusions suggest a kind of perverse insight into his own culpability, some reluctant awareness of a legacy of domination worthy of revenge. His paranoia seizes upon a figure of marked difference, and his racist and sexist, and later homophobic, epithets betray his acute anxiety—"That fat black bastard, that nasty black bitch over there, held his eye and nodded across the white heads of the other prisoners: *I'm gonna get you*" (553, original emphasis). Old age and illness have produced a leveling that terrifies and triggers a flailing, pathetic violence as Alfred attempts to defend himself against this would-be attacker: "He lunged as she came at him, but his belt had got stuck in the chair" (554). Alfred's unsuccessful struggle to free himself from the restraints confirms his absolute powerlessness: "Trying to work [his fingers] under the belt was so *obviously and utterly hopeless*—the belt had such overwhelming advantages of toughness and tightness—that his efforts soon became merely a pageant of spite and rage and incapacity" (554–55, original emphasis). Such hysterical rage is not uncommon in sufferers of dementia. One can only imagine the terror and confusion of such sudden strangeness, of being trapped in an unfamiliar and apparently threatening world. All of the narratives discussed in this chapter involve the eventual institutionalization of the afflicted person, but this move has very diverse effects. There is a degree of rage, even violent rage, experienced by Alfred, and to a lesser extent, Barney, that is not as apparent in Iris, Fiona, or Flo. For male sufferers of dementia, particularly for the Anglo-Saxon patriarch, Alfred, there is danger in confronting radical impermanence since such fluidity exposes the transience of his power and authority. As Alfred enters the space of illness, of old age, of difference, he experiences a loss of the prerogatives of strength and youth, race and class, that he cannot abide.

The various texts included in this chapter present a gendered vision of aging and later-life dementia, suggesting that the recognition of radical instability provokes different crises in men and women. Though aging may indeed initiate some neutralization, or at least subordination, of gender difference, as discussed earlier, these narratives of dementia and caregiving show that gender remains highly determinant in our experiences of aging and illness, a phenomenon discussed further in chapter 3. In *The Corrections,* Alfred's rage is largely the result of his suffocating dedication to conventionally masculine models of identity based primarily on exclusion and domination. This kind of imperial perspective means that his sense of self is devastated as he becomes a victim, a colonized other. Franzen's nonfictional account of his own father's dementia furthers such a patriarchal perspective: the only images of hope in the essay involve Franzen's final accounts of his father's "heroic" persevering power, the triumph of his father's "will" (34). The texts I discuss in this chapter suggest that the resilient cultural scripts of masculinity and femininity greatly determine both how "we" (the unafflicted) interpret victims of late-life dementia, and indeed how those victims experience their own disabilities. The moments of pleasure, even grace, afforded the afflicted characters in these stories and film are restricted to the female victims: Iris's solitary dance, Fiona's new love and sudden recognition, Flo and Rose's shared moment of humor. By contrast, each male sufferer responds with violence: at one point Barney smashes his face into a mirror (411), and Alfred struggles to attack his attendants.[23]

It appears in these texts that gender complicates the processes of witnessing, of collaboration and ethical responsibility. Patriarchal models of behavior inhibit some of the dialogic potential of caregiving: where Rose and Flo may experience a fleeting moment of levity that allows for a kind of communication and understanding that can accommodate difference, the father-son alliances in *Barney's Version* and *The Corrections* involve discrete individuals in distant dialogue.[24] Both *Barney's Version* and *The*

23. See also Caroline Adderson's *A History of Forgetting* for a rather melodramatic vision of dementia as a grotesque exaggeration of patriarchal violence. The afflicted character in that novel becomes suddenly anti-Semitic and homophobic, much like Alfred Lambert. Such constructions produce a highly symbolic version of aging and illness as the return of a kind of repressed primitive self, a vicious and destructive Id, unfettered by civilizing forces.

24. I am not suggesting that women are more *capable* of constructive collaboration. As Lorraine York points out in her study of women's collaborative writing, too often our interpretations of gendered collaboration have been colored by romantic visions of maternal kindness. York explains that "for the most part I have found a strong tendency to celebrate women's collaborations unproblematically and idealistically. This tendency is particularly strong in North America, home of influential feminist theories that see women as more other-directed and caring, and thus more given to relational ethics and collaborative problem-solving" (6). Though I do not subscribe to a model of untroubled fusion of subjects, I believe York's observation speaks to our expectations for, and even construction of, gendered collaboration. The idealization of women's

Corrections involve "corrections," though Michael Panofsky's pedantic footnotes are perhaps gentler than the resentment-fueled responses of the Lamberts to Alfred's disabilities. Nevertheless, as all of these narratives imply, there is a delicate balance necessary for respectful witnessing, a willingness to accept both the comprehensible *and* the incomprehensible, the familiar *and* the strange. In *Writing History, Writing Trauma* Dominick LaCapra proposes a particular definition of "empathy," one that refuses its common association with "identification or fusion with the other" (212). Instead, LaCapra contends that "empathy should rather be understood in terms of an affective relation, rapport, or bond with the other recognized and respected as other. It may be further related to the affirmation of otherness within the self—otherness that is not purely and discreetly other" (212–13). It is just this kind of difficult relation, and revelation, that later-life dementia can demand. In these fictional narratives, dementia poses serious challenges for both its victims and their empathetic witnesses (challenges further complicated by the demands of a patriarchal culture) as they struggle to maintain some sense of self in the face of such an acute demonstration of radical instability. Fictional representations of later-life dementia can reveal subjects confronting head-on the nonfixity of identity, the crude force of change that can make aging at once alarming, enlightening, and uncanny.

---

collaboration suggests that men's collaborative relationships are imagined as the antithesis, that is, as somehow inherently difficult and fraught. Whether intrinsic or not, the belief in the "naturalness" of women's collaboration and the challenge of men's greatly determines the operation of such partnerships. In novels such as *Barney's Version* and *The Corrections,* collaboration between men carries its own ideological baggage. In his treatment of male literary collaboration, Wayne Koestenbaum establishes the collaborative writer as one "who keenly feels *lack* or disenfranchisement, and seeks out a partner to attain *power and completion*" (2, emphasis added). He continues by proposing that post-1885 (the year of the Labouchère Amendment), collaboration "was a complicated and anxiously homosocial act" (3), claiming that "[c]ertain desires and dreads regularly follow in the double signature's wake: hysterical discontinuity, muteness, castratory violence, homoerotic craving, misogyny, a wish to usurp female generative powers" (4). York's and Koestenbaum's divergent critical strategies speak to the very different cultural scripts that often overdetermine the theory and practice of gendered collaboration, namely the assumption that women are cooperative and men combative. York often emphasizes conflicts in collaboration and the difficulty of fusion, while Koestenbaum is particularly interested in the subversive homoeroticism of men's collaboration, claiming that "men who collaborate engage in metaphorical sexual intercourse" (3). Though the collaborations in these texts are not explicitly engaged with questions of authorship, many of the same anxieties and difficulties plague the participants.

CHAPTER THREE

AGING, DOUBLES, AND THE MANIA OF DISSEMBLANCE

> *I at once realized to my dismay that the intruder was nothing but my own reflection.*
>
> —Freud, "The Uncanny" 371

> *I know what I look like—then I look in the mirror and don't look like that person. I think: "I don't know who that is."*
>
> —Julie Christie in Saga, April 2007

JULIE CHRISTIE'S comments articulate a curious yet common phenomenon in which the transformations of aging produce an unnerving double. Crises of recognition are not limited to those over sixty: explaining her use of Botox, forty-five-year-old actress Virginia Madsen has characterized such cosmetic procedures as attempts to rescue the true self that aging threatens to distort: "I am not using these injectables to look 25, I don't want to be 25. I just want to look like me" (qtd. in Silverman). Though the spectacle status of the actress's body undoubtedly amplifies the perils of aging, the problem of adjusting to a transformed image confronts any aging subject attentive to the ubiquitous cultural construction of aging as deformation. While the jarring effect of an unfamiliar, aged self can be experienced by men and women alike, the stakes may be higher for women when they contemplate their strangely new reflections in later life.

Profoundly familiar, yet strangely other, the figure of the double embodies the condition of uncanniness, provoking insecurity and dread in the "original" self who observes in his or her other a kind of doppelgänger.

With its attendant uncanniness, the double is integrally associated with the difficulties of temporal identity and not surprisingly appears frequently in narratives of aging. A common manifestation of the unsettling double is the startling, yet familiar, image of the aged self found in mirrors and photographs. Fiction and film involving older characters often include scenes of unsettling recognition during which older characters perceive an unexpected, yet strangely familiar, visage, an eerie double that is in fact an aged self.

In this chapter I review historical and critical accounts of the double in order to elucidate its long-standing association with mortality and to demonstrate how this association manifests the distinctly gendered meaning of aging. I follow this inquiry with an analysis of doubles in fiction by Alice Munro and P. K. Page and in the films *Requiem for a Dream* and *Opening Night*. In these texts, mirrors, windowpanes, and photographs provide glimpses of unexpectedly altered faces at odds with the similitude these characters take for granted. The shocking reflection dissolves the fantasy that selfhood can be shielded from age, confronting the subject with his or her own otherness. In various ways, these texts dramatize the sometimes violent clash of young and old selves as older characters are confronted by their time-altered image. Though both men and women are subject to the uncanniness of a persistently revising physical form, because of the association between female identity and corporeality in patriarchal culture, women experience aging into old age as a process of deterioration that, at its most extreme, can produce a kind of mania of dissemblance.[1] While my previous chapters suggest that the uncanniness of aging, of mutability, is not gender-specific, the suffering caused by such instability may be particularly acute for women whose youthful image becomes a specter of former

---

1. Woodward certainly does not deny the continuing importance of gender as one ages into old age. However, she does suggest that age eventually trumps other differences:

> [I]n advanced old age, age may assume more importance than any of the other differences which distinguish our bodies from others, including gender . . . in old age, and in our culture where aging is perceived negatively, old age becomes the dominant category to which we are consigned. If difference produces anxiety, what is the future of difference? For all of us, if we live long enough, that difference is constructed as old age. (*Discontents* 16)

My own argument is less exclusive. While old age befalls all of us, as Woodward asserts, the cultural resonances of "old man" and "old woman" are different. In the examples I gather in this chapter, gender is a forceful determinant in various female characters' experiences of aging.

fullness that haunts the supposedly deficient older self. This chapter continues and expands chapter 2's brief foray into gender concerns, providing a more detailed investigation into the repercussions of aging for subjects highly determined by physicality.

The double became a prominent literary trope in eighteenth-century gothic fiction, notably with the "doppelgängers" that appear in the novels of Jean Paul Richter, "'double-goers,' mirror-twisted twins without whom the other has neither past nor future, yet in whose present and presence tragedy must ensue" (H. Schwartz 64). But the concept of the double, of the uncanny figure that is so similar as to be frightening, has a much longer history. In their famous analyses of doubles, both Otto Rank and Freud embark upon an anthropological analysis that locates the power of the double in its "primitive" history, its prevalence and power in the myth and custom of various cultures, especially within indigenous communities. Freud collapses this cultural primitivism into psychological primitiveness, claiming that the power of the double, indeed, its very uncanniness, "can only come from the fact of the 'double' being a creation dating back to a very early mental stage, long since surmounted—a stage, incidentally, at which it wore a more friendly aspect. The 'double' has become a thing of terror, just as, after the collapse of their religion, the gods turned into demons" ("The Uncanny" 358). The terror of the double, according to both Freud and Rank, is its dual function as both protection against and confirmation of impending death. Building on Rank's analysis, Freud argues that within the narcissism of childhood, the double functions as "an insurance against the destruction of the ego, an 'energetic denial of the power of death'" (356), but once "this stage has been surmounted the 'double' reverses its aspect. From having been an assurance of immortality, it becomes the uncanny harbinger of death" (357). A confrontation with one's double is perhaps the ultimate uncanny experience, a disorienting, even destabilizing manifestation of the strangely familiar: the double is at once me and not me. The double assures me that I am at once *in here*, a conscious subject, and *out there*, an object gazed at by others. It signifies "man's eternal conflict, . . . the struggle between his need for likeness and his desire for difference" (Rank, *Beyond Psychology* 99). In its propensity to dissolve illusions of discrete, stable selfhood, the double exposes our own uncanniness, revealing the absolutely intimate as strange. Unlike the victim of dementia whose uncanniness may be othered, the uncanny double cannot be rejected, or even disavowed, for long, for he or she is always already within the subject: "One may want one's double dead; but the death of the double will always also be the death of oneself" (Royle

190). At once within and without, self and other, the double is uncanniness incarnate.

AGING DOUBLES, YOUTHFUL SELVES

In her insightful reading of Freud's theorization of aging, Kathleen Woodward situates aging in the discourse of uncanny doubles, arguing that the double's distressing effect is in fact the pain of the return of repressed embodiment. Woodward argues that in old age, "We say that our real selves—that is, our youthful selves—are hidden inside our bodies. Our *bodies* are old, *we* are not. Old age is thus understood as a state in which the body is in opposition to the self" (*Discontents* 62). She reads the problem of the image in old age as a reversal of the pleasure of the image in youth; in old age, "What is whole is felt to reside *within,* not *without,* the subject. The image in the mirror is understood as uncannily prefiguring the disintegration and nursling dependence of advanced age" (67, original emphasis). The double forces the subject to lay claim to strangeness, to recognize the other as in fact an uncanny self. The double shows the self its own age, what Richard Kearney calls the "dreaded alien" that is "*more like us than our own selves*" (*Strangers* 75, original emphasis). Aging can provoke a protective splitting that assists the subject in disavowing his or her temporality, but the aging self always returns, provoking startling, often disturbing confrontations with the constitutive instability of selfhood in the guise of the uncanny double.

In his extended examination of doubles, replicas, and imitations, Hillel Schwartz relates a case history from the 1920s that demonstrates doubling as a defense against the painful effects of mortality. In response to the trauma of death and aging, the patient enacted an absolute refusal of mortality, regarding all changes in those she loved as suspicious, even devious (73). Mme M.'s defensive strategy involved the fabrication of "*l'illusion des sosies,*" the belief that her children and husband had been kidnapped and replaced by pretenders (*sosies*) (Schwartz 73). As Schwartz explains, her *sosie* fantasy first appeared as a response to the death of four of her five children, allowing her to regard the deceased as only "unbreathing doubles" and her real children as alive but hidden (73). The fiction of substitutions, initially a protection against painful loss, next became an explanation for the changes of age when she refused to accept her remaining child and husband as real, claiming "that beneath the streets of Paris lay cellars in which were to be found more than two thousand of these missing children as well as the eighty *sosies* of her husband, who had been murdered years ago or who 'if in any event he is my husband, is more than unrecognizable, he has been totally transformed'" (73). For Mme M., both death and age were traumatic transformations that could be borne only by taking refuge in a fantasy of doubling and impersonation. Labeled "Capgras syndrome," after Jean Marie Joseph Capgras, Mme M.'s physician, this psychosis was a pathological demand for sameness and stability that speaks to the difficulty of absorbing the severe consequences of temporal identity, as Schwartz attests:

> [Capgras syndrome] was a disease of *chronic* exactitude, of double time. Each of us must admit that we are slightly older, slightly different each day. . . . The greater the exactitude of feature and character demanded of people over time, the more likely they will come to resemble "diverse apparitions of the same individual," doubles each a little off the original. Mme M. and Mme H. (another case written up in 1923) could accept their own timeliness and aging, but not that of their loved ones, whose features and characters had to be set in what to us must seem unreasonably permanent detail. All other appearances of their loved ones could only be facsimiles, never the real thing. (75, original emphasis)

Mme M. and Mme H.'s response to aging is unusual not just because of the failure to recognize changes in loved ones but also because of their consistent acceptance of alterations in their own images. Schwartz's comments recall Ricoeur's elucidation of temporal existence, in which the balance and incorporation of sameness and difference make continuity of identity possible. Identity and identification, the continuity of the subject, depend on "the ordered series of small changes which, taken one by one, threaten resemblance without destroying it. This is how we see photos of ourselves at successive ages of our life. As we see, time is here a factor of dissemblance, of divergence, of difference" (Ricoeur, *Oneself as Another* 117). But there are episodes in which the differences produced by temporality overtake the threads of continuity, producing, in the most extreme cases, a kind of mania, or psychosis.

The double embodies (quite literally) the troubling uncanniness of age, showing the subject a mortal self that he or she would prefer to deny. In fact, Freud's own account of his confrontation with the double, which he relegates to a footnote, is a narrative of unhappy aging. Banished to the margins of the essay, Freud's anecdote involves an unsettling encounter with his disavowed aged self, who appears as an unwelcome "elderly gentleman in a dressing-gown" entering his train compartment: "Jumping up with the intention of putting him right, I at once realized to my dismay that the intruder was nothing but my own reflection in the looking-glass on the open door. I can still recollect that I thoroughly disliked his appearance" ("The Uncanny" 371). Old age is an intruder, the unwelcome otherness of self transformed into disdained double. Here *recognition*, rather than misrecognition, generates the unhappiness of aging; as the initially alien image becomes increasingly familiar, the uncanniness of self becomes undeniable. The familiarity of the "elderly gentleman" prevents Freud from dismissing old age, from maintaining the protective fantasy of old age as a stranger who has "taken the wrong direction and come into my compartment by mistake." Invasive and unruly, age cannot be contained or controlled—it can never be "put . . . right," as Freud would like.

Another aside, this one from Rank's survey of the double, provides a compelling companion narrative to Freud's personal anecdote, shedding light on the function of gender in subject-image, or subject-double, relations. In a lengthy footnote to his chapter on narcissism and the double, Rank includes a chilling portrait of the dangerous power of the image for women in patriarchal culture. Rank relates how, in 1913 London, a lord was brought before the courts for punishing his "unfaithful sweetheart," Miss R., by locking her in "a room whose walls consisted of panes of plate glass" (73). The "sweetheart" was confined to this glass cell for eight days in an effort to enforce reflection and introspection, with the ostensible aim of putting the young woman on the path to self-improvement. Instead, the imprisoned woman was traumatized by the "horror of the ever-recurrent image of her own face" (73), which she eventually escaped through destruction, taking her fists to the panes of glass. Rank presents the details and interprets the motivations of the inmate's violent abolishment of her imprisoning image: "fragments were flying around and into her face, but she paid no heed to them; she kept on smashing, with only the purpose of no longer seeing the image of which she had conceived such a horror" (73). The collateral damage done to the woman's own face and hands speaks to the difficulty, for women, of safely abolishing the image. The burden of the ever-present image is inescapable, since to entirely refuse the image is, effectively, to refuse embodiment and risk destruction.

This footnoted narrative of a terrifyingly oppressive image, along with Freud's own anecdotal footnote, functions as a theoretical touchstone for my own investigation into the gendered function of the double in relation to aging. While Freud may have found his image disagreeable, his freedom to disassociate from such an image protects his authoritative subjectivity from the risks involved in confronting the double. As a controlling male narrator, Freud is able to confine his own distastefully mortal image to a footnote within a larger theoretical work, maintaining his disembodied, determining position within the main text. Such protection is unavailable to "Miss R.," who is instead doubly confined, both by the Lord's sadistic room of mirrors, and by Rank's narration, which maintains her as a marginal figure determined by her image, separated from the more masculine concerns afforded a place in the main body of the text.

MANAGEMENT AND MANIA
"Powers" and "A Kind of Fiction"

In fiction and film one finds similar scenes of delayed, and often dismayed, self-recognition by older characters. Mirrors and windowpanes provide glimpses of unexpectedly altered faces at odds with the similitude these characters take for granted. In stories by Munro and Page, confrontations with aged doubles further elaborate the gender concerns raised by Freud's and Rank's anecdotes of problematic reflections. Munro's story "Powers," from her 2004 collection *Runaway,* charts the protagonist's increasing self-estrangement as she ages, an estrangement that results in a mirror scene much like Freud's involving misrecognition and unhappy recognition. The story is divided into five sections, moving from Nancy's childhood in a small Ontario town, through her marriage and adulthood, to her solitary old age. The narration registers a growing estrangement in its shifting voice: while the opening section is a first-person account of Nancy's exuberant youth as recorded in diary entries, the following sections are told in a third-person voice increasingly removed from the earlier intimacy and energy. In the fourth section, the narrative introduces Nancy as an archetypal figure of age, opening with general remarks on location, period, season, and gender: "One late summer day in the early seventies, a woman was walking around Vancouver" (313). This style of undifferentiation continues for an entire page, the story's protagonist remaining only "a woman," a strange figure determined by her aged body: "She was sixty-seven years old, she was so lean that her hips and bosom had practically disappeared" (313). Her body is predominantly a signifier of age; the feminine characteristics of bosom and hips are conspicuous by their absence, drawing attention to this aged figure's gender.

The narration emphasizes her difference, one accentuated by her historical and geographic situation: "There did not seem to be a person within three decades of her age anywhere in sight" (313). The inappropriateness of her age is confirmed by the reproachful treatment of a boy and girl who sell her a "tiny scroll of paper" that, according to the boy, "contains wisdom" (313), a comment that undermines sentimental associations between old age and enlightenment. To the contrary, the young vendors make it clear that an old woman is in need of wisdom, the wisdom that only youth can provide.[2] Indeed, Nancy's refusal of their somber tone—she responds to their efforts at enlightenment with a joke—merely increases their reproach, causing the pair to "withdr[aw], in profound disdain and weariness" (313). Soon after, Nancy glimpses "an angry-looking, wrinkled-up, almost teary creature with thin hair" in a store window (314). Nancy's disdainful first response to her own reflection echoes Freud's contemptuous rejection of his "intruding" aged self; but, as with Freud, recognition eventually creeps into her evaluation of the stranger: "Dry-looking pale reddish-brown hair. Always go lighter than your own color, the hairdresser had said. Her own color was dark, dark brown nearly black. No it wasn't. Her own color *now* was white" (314, emphasis added). Aging deeply unsettles the illusion of stable selfhood as the transience of embodied identity asserts itself. Nancy must correct her own static definitions of selfhood by modifying her self-description: "Her own color now was white."

Nancy's survey of the visual faults of the "teary creature" in the window—"Somebody she didn't know and wouldn't want to know"—culminates in a reluctant avowal that, unlike Freud's self-recognition, depends on the potential for improvement and correction:

> It happens only a few times in your life—at least it's only a few times if you're a woman—that you come upon yourself like this, with no preparation. . . . But she had never had a jolt like this, a moment during which she saw not just some old and new trouble spots, or some decline that could not be ignored any longer, but a complete stranger. . . . She smoothed out her expression immediately, of course, and there was an improvement. You could say then that she recognized herself. And she promptly began to cast around for hope, as if there was not a minute to lose. She needed to spray her hair so it wouldn't blow off her face like that. She needed a more definite shade of lipstick. (314)

2. The dominance of youth culture in the 1970s is at least partly responsible for the young couple's smug dismissal of Nancy. But the scene does more than expose the intolerance of aging in a particular time and place. As I point out, the generalized description of the setting and characters, along with Nancy's own reaction to her reflection, suggest a wider notion of old age as foolish and deformed.

Just as Freud "thoroughly disliked his appearance," Nancy doesn't know, and more importantly "wouldn't want to know," this stranger so marked by "decline." This moment of uncanny confrontation depicts the transformations of age as not only distasteful, but offensive and desperately in need of correction. But unlike Freud, whose narrative of uncanny aging is merely an aside, allowing him to quickly recover from the shock of the double and return to his academic concern with the topic at hand, Munro's narrator, Nancy, is preoccupied with this alarming vision of uncanny selfhood. Freud's marginal narrative does not greatly affect his authoritative, disembodied narrative voice, and he remains a determining subject. Nancy's response is quite different. She immediately "cast[s] around for hope"—the strange double must be improved, made hospitable. The accoutrements of femininity (hairspray, lipstick, hair dyes) will help to make aging tolerable, will disguise and dampen the frightening strangeness of her image. Nancy's reaction speaks to a gendered tradition of correcting the unruly image; with increased age, the management of the image requires more labor. Here makeup is clearly what Patricia Mellencamp calls a tool of "remembrance," used to conserve and protect the original, that is, youthful identity (23). A belief in static selfhood, in alteration as disfigurement, confers on cosmetic masquerade a special power of restoration: "Restoration implies repossessing the original state of things, which is presumed to be the authentic state for all time. Aging is defined as a process of dispossession. Restoration is thus equated with rejuvenescence. If youth is natural, in the sliding economy of age, old age is unnatural and perhaps by extension even unlawful" (Woodward, *Discontents* 149). Nancy obeys the "law" by seeking to correct her disobedient image.

Nancy is not the only character in Munro's story to age from childhood to old age. The secondary characters, Tessa and Ollie, also experience the alterations of time. Nancy is a rambunctious girl living in a small town who finds herself unexpectedly engaged to the town doctor, Wilf Rubstone. Soon after the engagement Nancy meets Wilf's cousin, the tubercular Ollie, whose arrogance and loquaciousness set him apart from the taciturn doctor. In an effort to impress the worldly Ollie, Nancy takes him to visit Tessa, whose "powers" allow her to predict the contents of Ollie's pockets. "Old for her years, dishearteningly straightforward and self-contained" (290), Tessa both unsettles and fascinates Ollie, who eventually convinces her to leave her home and community to participate in scientific experiments in the United States. When funding for such research disappears, the pair make a meager living as traveling magicians. Nancy does not see Tessa again until many years later when she visits her in a private hospital. During their brief meeting, Nancy interprets Tessa's aging as a kind of intensification that has increased her strength and nobility, creating an impression of power quite unlike the withered image of Nancy's own aged body that appears later in the story:

> Tessa wasn't entirely gray. Her curls were held back in a tight net, show-ing her forehead unwrinkled, shining, even broader and higher and whiter than it used to be. Her figure had broadened, too. She had big breasts that looked as stiff as boulders, sheathed in her white baker's garb, and in spite of this burden, in spite of her position at the moment—bent over a table, rolling out a great flap of dough—her shoulders were square and stately. (306)

Tessa remains entirely recognizable, though altered. Time has merely exag-gerated her powerful aspect. The narrator's estimation of Tessa's stately, resilient physique, her empowerment over time, is set against Nancy's esti-mation of her own diminishment; "I'm surprised you knew me," she tells Tessa; "I've withered quite a bit since olden times" (306). Indeed, it is not long after that Nancy has trouble recognizing her own reflection in the Vancouver shop window.

Years later, at the story's conclusion, Nancy has a dream vision in which she sees Tessa's own troubled relationship with her mirror image. In her vision, Nancy imagines Tessa's growing unhappiness with a life of per-formance. Unlike Nancy, who looked to masquerade and performance as corrections that could provide relief, in Nancy's vision Tessa is sapped by illusion. Nancy imagines Tessa looking at her costumed self in the mirror of a dingy hotel room:

> Her skin is rouged now, but dull. Her hair is pinned and sprayed, its rough curls flattened into a black helmet. Her eyelids are purple and her eyebrows lifted and blackened. Crow's wings. The eyelids pressed down heavily, like punishment, over faded eyes. In fact her whole self seems to be weighted down by the clothes and the hair and the makeup. (331)

Makeup is no "remembrance" here; far from revealing and restoring the original, the true self, these cosmetics disfigure. In Nancy's image of Tessa, the accoutrements of masquerade are depressing, diminishing her self, her powers. This vision of a burdened and weakened Tessa speaks to the seem-ing purity that accompanies her powers. Part of her "power" is a kind of lucidity and truthfulness, both intellectual and visual: her body is straightforward, truthful *and* truth-telling. As a result, facades and masquerades appear as violations that obscure her mystically pure selfhood.

Nancy's dream offers a vision of resilience, of a fantastic woman for whom masquerade is unnecessary, a sturdy subject unthreatened by time. But such resilience is connected to her pathologized powers; in other words, the consequence of such potency is institutionalization and medical treatment. Tessa is not unchanged by time, but her alteration is a perversion of cultural scripts of aging in that she is somehow fortified or intensified by age, rather than diluted or damaged. This seeming imperviousness to scripts of aging and gender is part of Tessa's eccentricity, which titillates the more conventional Nancy. For Nancy, Tessa functions as a vision of age without dispossession, one without the need of management and correction. As such, Tessa becomes a fantastical double, one Nancy finds both marvelous and strange. Tessa is the story's overtly uncanny character, her apparent telekinetic abilities and her unconventional aging setting her apart from the more ordinary Nancy. But much like the mysterious and afflicted Fiona in "The Bear Came Over the Mountain," Tessa's opacity provokes the "normal," that is, nonpathological, protagonist's own awakening to uncanny selfhood. Tessa fails to be the story's reliable repository of otherness. Nancy eventually witnesses her own otherness in the uncanny double of her reflection, encountering what Richard Kearney calls the "ultimate stranger of strangers . . . the shadow of our own finitude" (*Strangers* 76). But as Nancy discovers, the aging stranger "she wouldn't want to know" cannot remain estranged for long; familiarity inevitably intrudes and the "complete stranger" (*Runaway* 314) is revealed as an uncanny double, the unbidden sign of her own uncanny temporality.

The shock and dismay of the double proves at least somewhat surmountable in Nancy's case. With the labor of adjustment and revision the initial threat posed by the altered, delinquent image can be neutralized. Like Freud, Nancy can endure an awareness of uncanny selfhood, though her endurance, unlike Freud's, depends on the prospect of correction. In both cases, initially shocking, then dismaying, the dawning awareness of dissembling selfhood troubles subjectivity without obliterating it. However, contemporary fiction and film often depict encounters with strange, temporal selves which produce a devastating shock that traumatizes the disavowing subject. P. K. Page's short story "A Kind of Fiction" rehearses such a process of debilitation as its protagonist, Veronika, gradually realizes that a frail old woman who evokes a startlingly intense empathy is, in fact, Veronika herself. In Page's story the lines between author and creation, young and old, self and other, blur to create an uncanny fluidity between entities. Veronika and a vulnerable old woman who falls at the story's start, and later shuffles from place to place with the help of a cane, function as multiple aspects of a self fractured by time. The old woman is a kind of ghost, always vanishing before Veronika can approach her. In a telling moment, Veronika attempts to talk to the woman, but the woman fails to respond: "Veronika wanted to speak to her, but as before the old woman didn't seem to see her, seemed in fact to give her powers of invisibility. Powers she didn't necessarily want" (10). The dubious powers of old age render Veronika imperceptible while this haunting old body remains visible. Unlike Munro's story, which raises the possibility of increased strength (Tessa's body) and ability (Nancy's visionary insight) with age, in "A Kind of Fiction" old age exerts a power *over* the protagonist, one that divides and diminishes her. For Veronika, the old woman is a corporeal specter, one that cannot converge with her own "unaged," that is, her not-yet-old, subjectivity. In other words, "A Kind of Fiction" reveals old age as entirely corporeal; old age is a frail, falling body, a disavowed body.

To preserve her subjectivity, Veronika cannot incorporate, or even recognize, her aged status. Indeed, the story's final revelation—that the old woman is in fact herself, her double—provokes a devastation very different from the irritation experienced by Freud in response to the "elderly gentleman." Veronika becomes distraught by the realization that she and the old woman share the same children and husband, a recognition that forces her to relive the losses and abandonments of these beloveds over time: "Veronika wept unashamedly as she walked, burdened by grief. . . . Veronika felt suddenly weak, barely able to walk, and her head was flooded with them all" (14). The revelation that the old woman's strangeness is in fact her own brings her to the brink of collapse: "She was dizzy and almost falling, her face wet from weeping" (14). Her uncanny knowledge of the pains and losses of the old woman's life move the protagonist closer and closer to a disorienting recognition, which finally comes at the story's close: "But the old woman—the old woman had been nameless. Veronika felt so weak she had to lean against a railing for support. She wondered if she were ill, gravely ill. Then suddenly as if struck by lightning, she knew the old woman's name. It was Veronika. Veronika Sylvia Ormond. Her own" (14). To recognize her own aging is to recognize her own otherness. For Veronika, the revelation of uncanny identity (she is the double and herself, both the old stranger and Veronika, both altered and the same) provokes a crisis, since incorporating the older double means accepting frailty, diminishment, an aberrant corporeality into her subjectivity.

AGING, GENDER, CINEMA

Throughout this book I have been treating uncanny aging as a human problem, but as these various examples demonstrate, age inevitably interacts with other categories of difference to produce divergent experiences of uncanny identity. Certainly women and men in the western world have different experiences of aging and old age.[3] Freud's own brief reference to an uncanny sex, to women's bodies as both familiar and strange, assumes a pre-existing female uncanniness that has implications for the uncanny insights provoked by aging. As Freud explains, female genitals constitute an "*unheimlich* place . . . the entrance to the former *Heim* [home] of all human beings, to the place where each one of us lived once upon a time and in the beginning" ("The Uncanny" 368). Such remarks buttress Jane Marie Todd's claim that in Freud's essay uncanniness is repeatedly gendered, concluding that, for Freud, "it is women who are *unheimlich*" (527). Such an interpretation of the female body is consistent with Freud's treatment of woman as inherently perverse. As Elisabeth Bronfen explains, according to Freud, "[w]oman functions as a privileged trope for the uncanniness of unity and loss, of independent identity and self-dissolution, of the pleasure of the body and its decay" (56). Freud's association of "woman" with uncanniness, and, as Bronfen points out, with death, places an exceptional burden on older women. The female body, already a sign of loss, according to psychoanalysis, becomes doubly afflicted in old age, making older women into prominent, even alarming, symbols of damage, both for others and for themselves. Working in a similar vein, feminist film critic E. Ann Kaplan claims that western culture produces aging as trauma for women, the result of "being *in time* and unable to get out of it" ("Trauma and Aging" 173). According to Kaplan, the trauma of aging arises from a confrontation with the inevitability of death, a confrontation that affects all humans but poses particular difficulties for women. Using Kristeva's theory of the abject, Kaplan explains that patriarchal culture dismisses old women because they "are what we have to push away from both the social body and even the individual body in order for that body

---

3. Popular culture provides endless instruction on the very different meaning of "aging" for men and women. Women's magazines, print and television advertising, film and television programming all dictate temporality as more relevant to women, who are constantly urged to resist and deny aging. For more detailed investigations into the mechanics and ramifications of gendered aging, see, for example, Woodward's *Figuring Age: Women, Bodies, Generations*, and Chivers's *Old Woman to Older Women: Contemporary Culture and Women's Narratives*.

to remain clean, whole, pure" (188). The intensity of the attention popular culture pays to female physicality produces problems for aging women, for whom the recognition of uncanny selfhood may indeed be so shocking as to jeopardize subjectivity. Fiction and film depict how the gendered strain of strangeness, the trauma of temporality, can fracture the female subject.

As in "A Kind of Fiction," the disintegration of boundaries between the non-old, familiar self and the aged stranger can enact a kind of trauma that leads to psychological breakdown, a disintegration of self literalized in Veronika's dizzied near-collapse. For many female characters in literature and film, divergence from a young image is a radical divergence from self, a loss of "correct" form that scrambles subjectivity. In contrast to the imperviousness of Mme M. and Mme H. to their own aging, their projection of temporal difference onto others, female characters in contemporary narratives often prove unable to deny their own otherness. For these characters, there can be no Ricoeurian balance between change and continuity. "The ordered series of small changes" enacted by time are refused; no "threat to resemblance" can be tolerated, and as a result, the inevitable return of disavowed mutability is devastating, producing a kind of mania of dissemblance. Theories of gender and image supplied by feminist film theory can assist one in understanding the significant threat posed by temporal dissemblance. A fundamental problem posed by the gendered cinematic image, for both performers and spectators, concerns proximity and identification. The long-standing association of woman with corporeality manifests itself in the iconic function of women in film. Narrative film at once exploits and reproduces a "claustrophobic closeness" between female subjects and images (Doane 24). In films such as *Requiem for a Dream* and *Opening Night,* viewers witness the prolonged disintegration of aging female characters who gradually succumb to mania in response to their confrontations with distressing difference. In both cases, the women experience a splitting of subjectivity that produces haunting doubles. But such divisions cannot be maintained, and the characters must submit to the disquieting knowledge that the double is indeed an aspect of uncanny selfhood.

Before turning to a detailed discussion of the gendered image, I must attend to the uncanniness of film itself. The visuality of film provides ample opportunities for exploring the consequences of the oppressiveness of the image and confounding doubling for aging women because, as Friedrich Kittler observes, film is itself a manifestation of doubles.[4] As a medium of

4. Kittler declares, "In order to catch sight of Doubles, people need no longer be either educated or drunk. Even illiterates, or especially they, see the student of Prague,

images, of uncannily spectral doubles, film is the medium par excellence for staging encounters with multiple selves. Cinema shares such a doubling effect with the photograph, which has a "dual identity as an icon, a bearer of resemblance, and as an index, a trace left by a past event" (Gunning 42). In his treatment of turn-of-century trick photography, Tom Gunning further explains that early photography itself "was experienced as an uncanny phenomenon, one which seemed to undermine the unique identity of objects and people, endlessly reproducing the appearances of objects, creating a parallel world of phantasmatic doubles alongside the concrete world of the senses verified by positivism" (42–43). Royle transfers such eerie powers of re-creation to cinema, declaring that "film is in its essence a world of doubles" (78). In its ability to make the past present, the cinema shares the photograph's uncanniness; as an "emanation of the referent" the photograph's liminality—referring at once to the past and the present—can enact a transformation of "subject into object" (Barthes, *Camera* 13). As a result, gazing at one's photographic image can produce a kind of vertigo,[5] "a faint uneasiness" (13), as one witnesses "the advent of myself as other: the cunning dissociation of consciousness from identity" (12). The photograph introduces us to our own difference.

Cinema alters the dynamic of the photograph by drawing our attention to temporality while at the same time satisfying our desire for stability in its presentation of images and events unfolding over time, but always in the same way. In its very medium film is both moving and static, a kind of archive in motion: the action is the result of thousands of tiny photographs skimming across a beam of light,[6] but these photographs are arranged in an unchanging sequence and the course of events is invariably the same. As a result, the action of film is ever moving, and yet always the same, unalterable. In this way film is somewhere between the absolute

his lover and his mistress—all Rank's 'shadowy, fleeting scenes,' which as such are already Doubles—as celluloid ghosts of the actors' bodies" (96).

5. In Hitchcock's film of the same name, "vertigo" is clearly linked to doubleness and death. The film's protagonist, Scottie, suffers from a debilitating vertigo that is apparently the result of a close encounter with mortality, one that leads to his partner's death. The prospect of his own death, one that has claimed his "double" instead, produces a pathological uneasiness, as expressed in the film's nightmare sequences, which represent Scottie's twisted psyche in surrealistic spirals and vivid colors. Of course the film's central mystery concerns the doubling of Madeleine/Judy (both played by Kim Novak), but it is Scottie's initial confrontation with his own otherness, his glimpse of his future status as corpse, that triggers the vertigo that the villain cunningly exploits with his manufactured double.

6. Digital technology alters the mechanics of film, which in turn alters its metaphorical resonance for aging.

fixity of a photograph and the constant change of a mirrored reflection. This status as both fixed and moving makes cinema particularly suited to the study of aging. Cinema is a dead fragment of the past like the photograph, yet capable of movement like the reflection, and this animation of the image leads us into a liminal space, lulls us into believing in its vitality, the reversal of photography's "disincarna[tion]" (Barthes, *Camera* 105). But because such vitality is so highly circumscribed, the actual bodies of actors are often strangely transformed over time when set against the preserved, yet animate, filmic image.

The rift between cinematic constancy and mortal transience that makes actors' actual bodies seem like imposters contradicting filmic truth can prove especially devastating for women. Cinema manifests the oppressive burden of the image for women that can make the unavoidable changes of age so debilitating (to both careers and psyches). The self-consciously aging "star"[7] protagonists of films such as *Sunset Boulevard* and *All About Eve* find themselves "marked by time twice over: as aging women they are marked as outside desire, and as aging stars, as image, they are both frozen and transitory" (Brooks 233). Feminist film criticism addresses the problem posed by cinematic visuality for women within patriarchal culture. According to Laura Mulvey, the dehumanizing condition of "woman as body" is largely inescapable in narrative films, which rely on women connoting "*to-be-looked-at-ness*" for the endowment of audience pleasure (33). In her groundbreaking article on gendered visual pleasure, Mulvey explains how narrative film typically codes men as active agents furthering

---

7. The public response to the film "star" exposes a desire to maintain the limited temporality of cinema. As Richard Dyer explains, "Stars not only bespeak our society's investment in the private as the real, but also often tell us how the private is understood to be the recovery of the natural 'given' of human life, our bodies" (13). But, of course, stars cannot be *too* "real" or they lose their iconic status. The collapse of the public and private in the "star" creates an untenable position: the figure must be at once mythic and human, celluloid and corporeal, timeless and mortal. It is notable that Dyer's analysis of the significance of "heavenly bodies" singles out three for attention: Marilyn Monroe, Paul Robeson, and Judy Garland. In each case study the star is investigated as a sign of difference, of gender, ethnicity, and sexuality, respectively. The untenable "star" position is perhaps most damaging for women, predisposed as they are to visual overdetermination. In narrative cinema, the persistent coding of women as empty signifiers, as fetishistic objects of desire, is a serious impediment to female performers, since their temporality puts them at odds with the iconic image required of the "star." As a result, female film actors often speak of careers impaired by age, their faces and bodies perceived as increasingly unsuitable for public consumption over time. See, for example, the personal narratives supplied by numerous actresses over the age of forty in the film *Searching for Debra Winger*.

the narrative, while women remain passive objects of the gaze that arrest narrative action. Though Mulvey's polemical text has been criticized for its rigid, psychoanalytic categorization of gendered spectators and images, the basic problem of female objectification and fetishization, of "Woman as Image, Man as Bearer of the Look" (Mulvey 33), remains central to discussions of women and film. These very gendered politics of the image are undeniable; despite shifting representational strategies and the variable meanings afforded "woman," based on the interaction of difference, narrative films, particularly Hollywood films, continue to engage female bodies primarily as sites for visual pleasure.

In her article on women and the masquerade in film, Mary Ann Doane draws on Joan Riviere's work to elaborate the problematic cultural association between women and bodies, a process of reduction that inhibits female spectators from obtaining adequate distance from the cinematic image. Drawing on Freud's use of the hieroglyphic as a metaphor for femininity, Doane interrogates the simultaneous overpresence and absence of "woman" in film: "the hieroglyphic is the most readable of languages. Its immediacy, its accessibility are functions of its status as a *pictorial* language, a writing in images. For the image is theorized in terms of a certain *closeness,* the lack of a distance or gap between sign and referent" (18). This problematic proximity, this "overpresence of the image," that makes women in film at once mysterious and intrinsically legible, leads to a degree of gendered uncanniness in narrative film. Cinema makes "woman" as image particularly uncanny—familiar, yet enigmatic—just as images of women exaggerate the underlying uncanniness of cinema. The proliferation of uncanny potentials—uncanny visual reproduction, uncanny gender, uncanny temporality—produces a highly volatile situation for older women contemplating their own cinematic and photographic images.

MENACING TRACES
Specters of Youth in
Requiem for a Dream and *Opening Night*

The film *Requiem for a Dream,* directed by Darren Aronofsky, capitalizes on this volatility in its depiction of the disorienting "that-has-been"-ness of the photograph (Barthes, *Camera* 77), aggravated by the gendered burdens of aging. Consisting of three interrelated narratives, *Requiem for a Dream* follows four characters who suffer calamity as a result of addiction. While the young characters, Harry, Marion, and Tyrone, succumb to heroin addiction in their attempts to make a fortune dealing narcotics, Harry's lonely mother, Sara Goldfarb, falls victim to the prescription diet pills she ingests in an attempt to recapture the lost body of her youth, figured, significantly, in an old photograph of a younger, thinner Sara in a vibrant red dress. In Aronofsky's cinematic treatment, Sara's confrontation with her own alterity via the vertiginous past-ness of the photographed self initiates a struggle against change, a denial of the difference of self that dismantles her subjectivity. Eventually, Sara's efforts to banish the disobedient double, that is, her own reflected body, and to restore her youthful, photographed self, through medication and severe dieting, produce a psychological crisis that necessitates institutionalization, and finally electroconvulsive therapy.

Sara Goldfarb's loss of agency as pathological inmate is the culmination of her lonely existence as "cultural refuse" (Brooks 233), her only company an aggressively patronizing television self-help guru, and the similarly discarded older female tenants of Sara's apartment building. Aronofsky depicts this gaggle of old women in a caricature of "biddyness"; sunbathing in their folding chairs outside the apartment building, they cluck and coo at the arrival of a letter announcing the possibility that Sara will be invited to appear on the self-help television show. The women appear as an undifferentiated mass, determined only by their age and gender; their excitement at the form letter speaks to both their naïveté and their desperation. The news is regarded as a chance for Sara to reclaim the coveted position of desired object, and there is general agreement that her body must be adjusted, her aging corrected to properly fulfill the role. The photograph of Sara is an artifact, evidence of a young, vital, attractive past self that accentuates the loneliness and bodily transformation that have come with time.[8] The red dress worn in the photograph becomes a fetish, coming to represent the elusive happiness of the past, the glory of a pre-aged self. The photograph, and by extension, the red dress, divide Sara: the photograph's haunting reminder of the self that "has been" is set against the distressing image reflected in mirrors. Sara's obsessive desire to wear the red dress is a desire to undo time, to return to the past, an impossible desire that the prescribed weight-loss amphetamines are meant to enable. In the end, the strain of refusing the mirror image in favor of the photographic one is debilitating. In her efforts to reverse the photo's oth-

8. In the photograph, Sara is flanked by her son, Harry, and a man one can assume to be her husband. In the present, Sara lives alone, abandoned by such male company.

Figure 1
Sara's exaggerated make-up and hair color create a parody of youthful attractiveness. (Still taken from *Requiem for a Dream* provided through the courtesy of Lionsgate)

ering, that is, to make the *reflection* her double, and the *photograph* her authentic self, Sara suffers delusional anxiety and psychotic breakdown.

The film emphasizes the hopelessness of Sara's efforts to recapture lost youth in its depiction of a delusional Sara primping in front of the mirror, her hair dyed a clownish orange, bright red lipstick smeared on and around her lips, her eyelids painted with garish blue eyeshadow and thick layers of mascara (see figure 1). In adopting grotesquely exaggerated makeup and hair color in order to perform the self she wishes to reclaim, Sara instead becomes a parody of youthful attractiveness. Finally able to fit into the red dress, Sara has already succumbed to the mania of dissemblance; her application of clownish makeup recalls Bette Davis's perverse masquerade of youthfulness in *Whatever Happened to Baby Jane?* Sara's performance in front of the mirror betrays the perverse "success" of her transformation: her psychosis has permitted the cohabitation of past and present, allowing the photographic and reflective selves to merge. Such convergence comes at a price—Sara is removed from the spectator's reality, inhabiting the place of pathological victim, entirely strange. In her refusal of the uncanniness of temporal subjectivity, that is, of aging, of change, Sara moves into the space of absolute otherness, becoming an alien figure, a caricature of insanity.

Sara's efforts to regain youth stem from a desire to "appropriately" fashion herself for the spectatorial gaze. She has, of course, been trying to lose weight with the hope of appearing on a television show, the impossibility of an older woman occupying the role of feminine object lending a futility to her struggle. The character of Sara in *Requiem for a Dream*

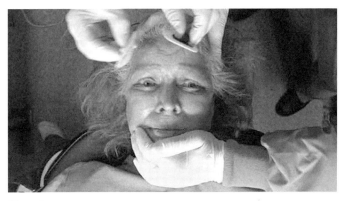

Figure 2
The abjection of old age: Sara's desire for a youthful body via diet pills leads to institutionalization. (Still from *Requiem for a Dream* provided through the courtesy of Lionsgate)

can only be an object of pity or disgust, and the place of the erotic object is occupied by the younger characters, particularly Marion, whose young, naked body is repeatedly fetishized in static shots and close-ups. *Requiem for a Dream* relies on the abjection of gendered old age for much of its drama, including scenes of psychosis, nightmarish hospital wards, and a grisly ECT episode (see figure 2). The film charts a path between aging and insanity that suggests a direct correlation between the two; plagued by the taunting image of a past self, Sara makes every effort to banish the perverse, aged self that greets her in the mirror. *Requiem for a Dream* shows an awareness of the marginalization of older women as abject, but exploits the pathos of this abjection, depicting Sara as a pitiable victim at the mercy of the weapons of patriarchal culture: pharmaceuticals and television, medical professionals and institutions. Yet despite Sara's apparent victimization, the film implicitly holds her responsible for her own downfall, since her own simplicity allows the various oppressive forces to be so destructively effective. Not long after the delusions have begun, she explains to Harry that the prospect of appearing as an object of beauty on television gives her a reason to get up in the morning: "What have I got, Harry? Why should I even make the bed or wash the dishes? I do them. But why should I? I'm alone. Your father's gone, you're gone. I got no one to care for. What have I got, Harry? I'm lonely. I'm old. . . . I like thinking about the red dress and the television and you and your father. Now when I get the sun I smile." Sara is largely a victim in Aronofsky's film, of doctors, of age, but primarily of her own desire for youth.

Filmmakers have often capitalized on the exaggerated uncanniness of older women in scenes of terror and horror. Films such as *Rosemary's Baby* and *Whatever Happened to Baby Jane?* depend on the abjection of older women, their consignment to the realm of the "monstrous feminine," Barbara Creed's term for "what it is about woman that is shocking, terrifying, horrific, abject" (1). "Monstrous feminine" figures include, among others, the witch, "invariably represented as an old, ugly crone who is capable of monstrous acts" (2). If in psychoanalytic terms older women are doubly uncanny, the uncanniness of cinema further intensifies this alterity, making aging film actresses triply "afflicted." As a result, films about aging actresses provide a surfeit of uncanny interactions as characters confront the consequences of a career, indeed an identity, based on a static image.

John Cassavetes' *Opening Night* confronts the traumatic consequences of such manifold uncanniness in its portrayal of an actress suffering the effects of a career as a public image, depicting in bleak terms the difficulty created by her conflicted status as at once iconic and temporal. The film both critiques and exploits the repercussions of a culture that transforms temporal subjects into static symbols. *Opening Night*'s self-reflexive attention to the demands and risks of performance dramatizes the many difficulties confronting an aging actress, in particular, the splitting of self between lost, glorious youth and diminished, degraded old age. Myrtle (played by Gena Rowlands) is preparing to star in the play *The Second Woman*, which concerns a character, Virginia, entering the dreary "second" phase of life, the difficult transition from erotic object to cultural refuse.[9] Myrtle resists the despair and degradation the role of Virginia demands, sparking an ongoing debate between herself and the play's sixty-

9. Though the film does not provide a complete sense of the play's narrative, it clearly involves Virginia's morose contemplation of her life, past and present. Virginia visits her ex-husband, who has remarried and now has several children, a visit that precipitates various conflicts, between her previous husband and his new family as well as between Virginia and her current husband, Marty. Early on in *Opening Night* viewers witness the rehearsal of a scene between Virginia and Marty that foregrounds the differences, and conflict, between the "first" and "second" women, that is, between women young and old, as Marty discusses his career as a photographer. "Did you see my kid?" Marty asks Virginia. "Ain't she beautiful? . . . I'm giving up older people," Marty tells her; "You can't photograph them without their clothes on." Nonetheless, he goes on to explain the benefits of old age: "You know why I love older people? Because they know everything. But they don't show that they know everything. I can stand here and I can look at this woman, this old lady [pointing to large portrait], and I can count every wrinkle on her face. And for every wrinkle there's a pain, and for every pain there's a year, and for every year there's, there's a person, there's a death, there's a history, and there's a kindness. Now you look at this kid over here, she's not kind." Marty confirms the body-subject division between young and old: the young woman is an erotic spectacle, but cruel, the old woman a historic site, wise and kind, but asexual.

five-year-old author, Sarah Goode. Rehearsing a scene in which Virginia is slapped by her husband, Marty, Myrtle refuses to tolerate the violence the script demands, responding to the attempted slap with screams, laughter, and by striking back at Maurice (the actor playing Marty). From the stage, Myrtle voices her discomfort with the role, and Sarah explains Virginia's sad motivations: "This woman you're playing is as helpless as you are, and as helpless as I am," she tells Myrtle. "She has no weapons. She wants to fall in love, but her time has passed. It's too late, it's as simple as that. You understand that part of it, don't you?" But Myrtle repeatedly resists the hopelessness the play associates with aging. Her resistance becomes a larger refusal of aging and change; when Sarah attempts to position Myrtle herself as a "second woman" by repeatedly inquiring about her actual age, Myrtle evades the question through silence and diversion. But Myrtle's resistance to the role of Virginia, and by extension, to aging itself, has serious personal ramifications as the increasing external pressure to confront her own temporality strains her subjectivity to the point of fracture, signaled by the appearance of increasingly menacing visions of a familiar, but lost, youthful self.

It is notable that critical treatments of *Opening Night* often banish aging to the periphery of the discussion (King, Carney, Berliner). For example, Homay King dismisses aging in the film as "a metaphor for a shutting down of affective mortality" (110). Such a critical marginalization of aging threatens to duplicate the very dismissal that Myrtle fears as an aging woman and as an actress. King implies that aging naturally involves lessening, a "shutting down." But such narrowing of potential and possibilities is not merely an effect of aging itself, and King overlooks the oppressive cultural forces that threaten Myrtle's selfhood by restricting her to static symbols. Some critics do attend to the film's central preoccupation with aging. In her analysis of the film, for example, Jodi Brooks speaks to the enforcement of loss that confounds Myrtle: "In a state of shock, Myrtle tries to find a way of locating herself in relation to discourses of desire. . . . Her dilemma, then, is to find a way of producing an image of women and aging in which she can locate herself—and which doesn't send the middle-aged woman to the wings" (238). Far more than metaphorical, aging has serious repercussions that throw Myrtle into crisis, as her own temporal identity comes into conflict with the static images provided by her profession.

In its self-conscious attention to the plight of the aging female star, *Opening Night* dramatizes the clash between stasis and change aggravated by cinema. Cinema purports to incorporate temporality in its rapid projection of static images. But the falseness of filmic vitality is exposed in *Opening Night*'s opening collage, which draws attention to the photographic still at the heart of the cinema. Immediately following a brief scene of the "real" Myrtle taking a quick drink and smoke before her entrance onstage, *Opening Night* shows cutout stills of Myrtle-the-actress onstage before a darkened audience. We hear the appreciative audience, but see only stasis and artifice. Myrtle's voice-over narration speaks to the alienation of aging, which aggravates the division between icon and subject: "When I was 17 I could do anything. It was so easy. My emotions were so close to the surface. I'm finding it harder and harder to stay in touch." These introductory images of dramatic artifice establish a conflict between intense, authentic youth and alienated age that becomes increasingly acute as the film continues.

Soon after the scene of still images ends, Myrtle comes face to face with the emotional intensity of youth that the voice-over narration mourned. After a preview production of *The Second Woman* in New Haven, Connecticut, Myrtle is engulfed in a throng of young female fans as she exits the theatre. One girl in particular draws her attention, a young blonde woman whose adoration reaches an ecstatic pitch. In her near-delirious attestation of love for Myrtle, she wraps her arms around the actress's neck, and Myrtle asks the girl's name and age, discovering that she is a seventeen-year-old named Nancy. During this exchange, the medium close-up shows Myrtle and Nancy in close profile, their faces mere inches from one another. They appear as twins, both wearing dark clothes that accentuate their white-blonde hair. Ushered into a waiting car, Myrtle and the play's cast and crew watch as Nancy presses herself to the car window in the rain, the tightening frame reducing her to a wet blur. As their car drives away the young woman's delirious devotion results in a fatal accident; she is so transfixed that she moves into the path of an oncoming car.

Not long after, the deceased young fan begins to appear to Myrtle, initially as a comforting embodiment of the young, vital self she has lost, the seventeen-year-old who "could do anything," whose "emotions were so close to the surface." But the consolation of the double soon turns to threat as Myrtle's visions of Nancy become increasingly sinister, even violent. In a disturbing scene of apparent self-flagellation, Myrtle suffers the outrage of her spectral double, her head bashed repeatedly into a doorframe. However, unlike the previous episodes involving the return of the young fan in which Nancy is visible to both Myrtle and the spectator, here she remains invisible and Myrtle appears as both victim and perpetrator, smashing her own face against the doorjamb. The horror of Myrtle's situation is fully apparent: whether haunted or delusional, she is the aging victim of lost youth, punished for her temporal condition on a variety of fronts. Myrtle is at risk at every level of *Opening Night*'s multiple realities: offstage, Myrtle is plagued by the ambitious, aggressive specter of youth; onstage, her playwright and director insist that she "act" her age, enforcing age as defeat.[10] It is notable that the double's violence coincides with Myrtle's implicit submission to the discouraging premise of Sarah's play. The abuse occurs not long after Sarah takes Myrtle to a spiritualist to confront the dangerous ghost, and Myrtle adopts the play's thesis to explain her predicament: "The play we're doing now is about the gradual lessening of my power as a woman as I mature. At some point in life youth dies and the second woman in us takes over. I believe that Nancy is the first woman in my own life." "The Second Woman," both the specter and the play, takes Myrtle hostage, forcing her to submit to the cultural construction of aging as disintegration and deformation.

In the end, Myrtle must destroy the threatening image of youth that haunts her, beating the phantom to the ground with her fists in order to escape (see figure 3). This obliquely self-destructive violence, the annihilation of a representation, recalls the imprisoned victim of the vengeful lord in Rank's narrative. For both these women, such self-destruction is a means to liberation, albeit a dubious one since their "emancipation" requires sacrifice: the young woman of Rank's narrative is wounded by broken glass, while Myrtle is propelled into a perilous drinking binge that leaves her delirious, barely able to stand or speak. She takes the stage nonetheless, producing her own version of the play by improvising its final scene. In the film's final act Myrtle appears to re-emerge from the nadir, scarred, but triumphant. Her manipulation of the play is a resounding success. After she destroys her double, Myrtle "kills" Virginia, replacing the fading and hopeless character Sarah has written with an alternate of her own making that acknowledges the absurdity of uncanny identity and transforms melodrama into comedy. In effect, Myrtle develops a subject position that incorporates difference without slipping into complete alienation. In the end it is an *acceptance* of uncanniness and absurdity, of the multiplicity of identity, that protects Myrtle from further disaster. Her improvisation of the play's final scene directly addresses the alterity of selfhood through parodic exaggeration that undermines the script's gendered angst. Myrtle's

10. There is yet another metatextual level of victimization if one considers the risks (both personal and professional) posed to Gena Rowlands in performing Myrtle/Virginia. As Myrtle, Rowlands performs the very age-related psychological crisis that her character resists for its hopelessness and potential impact on her career as an actress.

Figure 3
Myrtle beats her double, the threatening image of youth that haunts her. (Still from *Opening Night*, courtesy of Westchester Films)

performance employs comedy as resistance according to models offered by Kathleen Rowe, who investigates the "unruly woman," as "an ambivalent figure of female outrageousness and transgression with roots in the narrative forms of comedy and the social practices of carnival" (10).[11] Myrtle's substitution of parody for scripted suffering enacts such a resistance; by self-consciously addressing the difficulties and pains of aging that defeat Virginia, Myrtle is able to temper their effect.

This is not the first time Myrtle has altered the script during the performance, but in the past her costars have resisted her changes, making every effort to steer the dialogue back to the script. During the opening night performance, however, Myrtle's costar (and former lover), Maurice, who plays Virginia's current husband, Marty, responds to Myrtle's changes in the spirit of the improvisation, complementing Myrtle's comedic treatment of the baffling uncanniness of identity. Their absurd conversation exposes the daunting multiplicity produced by temporality, and by performance. "Well I am not me. I used to be me. I'm not me anymore," Maurice/Marty tells Myrtle/Virginia, explaining further: "We are absolutely different people than we were. When I look at my face in the mirror when I'm shaving in the morning, you know what I see? I can see it then in my face. It's hard

---

11. Rowe explicitly connects the unruly woman with age and other "excesses": "The unruly woman . . . often makes a spectacle of herself with her fatness, pregnancy, age, or loose behavior" (33). Indeed Rowe opens her book with reference to Bakhtin's treatment of a sculpture of "senile, pregnant hags" (2), an image that encapsulates the transgressive unruliness of conflating life stages.

to cover it up. There's something deeply cynical about my face. It's hard to cover it up." Marty smirks as he repeats these final lines with parodic vigor and volume, and the audience responds with hearty laughter. "My heart pounds. My stomach is empty and I feel like screaming. I am restless with this pose," he says. "Well I'm not me," Myrtle/Virginia drawls, her tone one of exaggerated nonchalance. "And I know that I am someone else," Maurice/Marty replies. Myrtle/Virginia concludes by offering a dispassionate account of their replacement, treating the newness of the "aged" self as a perverse joke: "It's definite then. We've been invaded. There's someone posing here as us." Delivered with parodically exaggerated stage movements and smiling glances at the audience, these lines dissolve multiple boundaries of identity and reality, breaking divisions between old and young, actor and role, performance and reality.

By admitting the uncanny double into the territory of the self, Myrtle resists the traumatic fracture that culture demands, that is, the splitting of self into lost youth and mournful old age. By concluding the play with self-conscious comedy about aging and the "stranger within," Myrtle and Maurice are able to maintain a liminality that the division of Virginia into "first" and "second" women refused. Rowe claims that "[a]ll narrative forms contain the potential to represent transformation and change, but it is the genres of laughter that most fully employ the motifs of liminality" (8). In the improvisation of *The Second Woman*, laughter opens a space for contradiction and difference without resolution. Within the liminal space between age and youth, performance and reality, Myrtle/Virginia exposes the absurdity of these divisions, attesting to the uncanniness of identity in a parodic deadpan delivery that undermines the melodramatic violence and despair of both *The Second Woman,* and *Opening Night* itself. Myrtle's improvisation (and by extension, Gena Rowlands', since the scene itself was apparently the result of improvisation between Rowlands and her coactor, Cassavetes, who played Maurice/Marty) develops parodic comedy as a way out of the dreary scripts of aging, replacing the pathos of Virginia's victimization with absurd dialogue, the humiliating slap with subversive slapstick.

It is no coincidence that Myrtle's final triumph occurs onstage. The final performance of *The Second Woman* allows for a circumscribed spontaneity, an exhibition of one-way temporality within the larger frame of endlessly repeatable cinematic representation. In other words, the success of Myrtle's improvisation depends upon the film audience's belief in the play's demonstration of human time, that is, linear, one-way time that precludes second takes. The play-within-the-film conceit draws further attention to the central friction between stasis and change in *Opening Night*. It is only on stage that the liminality produced by aging can be confronted. At once honest and artificial, improvised and planned, fleeting and preserved, the filmed play draws attention to the problematic rift between human and cinematic temporality.

The revised *Second Woman* concludes with a strange, shared trick in which Myrtle/Virginia and Maurice/Marty reach to touch foot-to-foot as they pass one another, a bizarre, comedic action that allows for equal participation (see figure 4). This final physical gag symbolizes the potentials of the new model of relations the actors have created. The curtains falls on their gag, producing an unresolved conclusion, a cohabitation of opposites and contradiction that the original *Second Woman* could not abide. Much like the final nonsensical scene in Munro's "Spelling," the tolerance of absurdity and a certain degree of incomprehensibility (if only momentarily) defuses the threat of the uncanny. Rather than reading the strangeness of self as a consequence of the many tragic losses of aging, as does Sarah's script, Myrtle and Maurice's comedic revisions interpret the strangeness of self as a bizarre newness, as multiplication rather than mere disintegration. No longer simply menacing, the double produced by aging is ridiculous, bizarre, even preposterous, but always part of the subject. Furthermore, the circumstances of the scene's development add a metatextual, liberatory potential, allowing the actors themselves (Rowlands and Cassavetes) to become active participants. This final, apparently improvised scene,[12] performed for a live audience of voluntary extras, frees actress Gena Rowlands from the often destructive demands of both the diegetic scripting of Myrtle as Virginia by Sarah, and the arguably even more harrowing scripting of Rowlands as Myrtle by the writer-director, Cassavetes. The film's concluding improvisational comedy trades the earlier scenes of violence (the rehearsal of the slap, the bashing of Myrtle's head against the doorframe, the striking of the haunting double, Nancy) for a scene of parody and laughter that facilitates simultaneous tolerance and resistance: toler-

---

12. In an interview included on the Criterion DVD release of the film, Ben Gazzara and Gena Rowlands discuss the unusual circumstances of the scene's development. According to Gazzara, even the other actors were unaware of what the final scene of *The Second Woman*'s "opening night" performance would look like, and Rowlands insists that she and Cassavetes had not rehearsed the scene prior to their improvisation in front of the voluntary live audience. Regardless of the degree of spontaneity—critics have amended Cassavetes' claim of total improvisatory scripting and performance in his films (Berliner and King)—the scene includes significant creative participation by Rowlands.

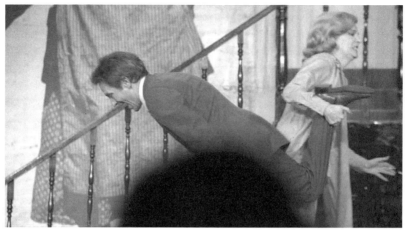

Figure 4
Myrtle and Marty's bizarre foot-grabbing finale to the play. (Still from *Opening Night*, courtesy of Westchester Films)

ance of the strangeness of temporality, resistance to the cultural scripting of that strangeness as a dangerous, even perverse, deficiency.

By inhabiting the supposedly perverse, "unruly" position of "aged" woman, and rewriting the interpretation of such a position to incorporate the humor of uncanny change, there is the potential for resistance and empowerment, for the "hope" that Myrtle complained was missing from Sarah's play. *Opening Night,* along with "Powers" and "Spelling," suggests that *embracing* the strange or absurd may be the only "solution" to the vexing instability of temporal identity. Notably, in all three cases, it is women's experiences of aging that initiate the incorporation of nonsense and absurdity. Though Maurice participates wholeheartedly in the final comedic improvisation, it is Myrtle's struggles that are galvanizing; left unharassed, Maurice would adhere to Sarah's script (which does not punish his character for aging). For his character, Marty, aging means no loss of power or selfhood. He remains an active, determining subject throughout the play, making judgments on women old and young, pronouncing older faces superior for their authenticity and wisdom. In Sarah's script Marty does the slapping and Virginia gets slapped. Though aging is undeniably universal, its interaction with other forms of difference determines the severity of its repercussions.

In both *Opening Night* and *Requiem for a Dream* there is a condensation of difference as gender and aging coalesce, provoking disturbing, violent confrontations with uncanny identity. In these films, the aging woman's specular achievements—Myrtle Gordon's star status, Sara Gold-farb's photographic youthful splendor—are threatened by the alterations of time. For Sara there is no escape, no possibility of laughter. Indeed, the only laughter in the film is at her expense when she imagines the talk-show audience in her living room, hooting and giggling at her attempts to restore her lost youth. Sara's parodying of herself is unwitting and destructive; what she sees as recaptured splendor the taunting audience perceives as grotesque masquerade. The grotesque is never far from women's comedy, since both involve an overturning of patriarchal expectations: "the unruly woman often enjoys a reprieve from those fates that so often seem inevitable to women under patriarchy, because her home is comedy and the carnivalesque, the realm of inversion and fantasy where, for a time at least, the ordinary world can be stood on its head" (Rowe 11). Comedy may provide resistance and relief, but only "for a time." So where is the aging, female subject left after this temporary respite? What does she do when the laughter ends? The final moments of *Opening Night* hint at a possibility. When the curtain comes down and the laughter fades, Myrtle no longer looks amused. Without an audience she is alone with her own absurdity, her potential monstrosity as *aged* object. But the film's final moments involve an interaction between Myrtle and the director's wife, Dorothy Victor, who up until this moment has appeared only in relation to her husband. "Lady, it's a privilege," she says, embracing Myrtle. The film ends by freezing this image of union, the credits transposed over the embrace. The emphasis on the embrace suggests that Myrtle's parody and laughter has reached Dorothy, an audience member, raising the possibility of an alliance that excludes the film's manipulative male characters, such as Myrtle's domineering director, Manny Victor, and her resentful costar, Maurice.

AGING, DIFFERENCE, DOUBLES

Doubles present subjects with their strange corporeality, their own otherness. Patriarchal constructions of gender can seriously aggravate the difficulty of apprehending and acknowledging the uncanny identity the double represents. The textual examples included in this chapter demonstrate a variety of responses to the shocking image of an aged self: denial, correction, despair, even mania. Though the severity differs, all these responses share an element of refusal. Whether wishing to revise the image like Nancy in "Powers" or Sara Goldfarb in *Requiem for a Dream*, or rejecting it outright like the protagonists in "A Kind of Fiction" and *Opening Night,* all these characters share a motivating intolerance for their own image. The pain of difference can entangle, or even snap, the threads of continuity, making the aging self a threatening other that must be refused at all costs. These characters reveal how in aging the remembered former self appears more real and more authentic than the embodied self captured in reflections. In other words, the subject comes to view herself as a counterfeit double set against the lost true self of youth, a perspective aggravated by the filmic reification of female subject as image. The risks of such counterfeiting are numerous, and the alternatives can be difficult.

Opening Night suggests that laughter may assist one in tolerating the multiplicity and mutability of uncanny temporality. But of course constant laughter is its own form of mania. So how to abide the difficulties of aging between bouts of laughter? Munro's "Powers" may provide the least desperate portrait of aging in Nancy's irony and humor, her begrudging recognition of the absurd double, her late-life development of visionary powers, if only imaginary. Nancy tolerates the shock of the unexpected reflection and is able to turn away from such images in order to focus on interior visions. These may be insights to hope for and work toward: to acknowledge the uncanniness of identity as unsettling and bewildering, as absurd and even outrageous, while resisting the urge to consign the strange image of aging to the realm of frightening alterity. Perhaps, at times, one can perceive the aging double without anxiety or resentment. Comedy confirms that such a reaction is indeed possible. The double-edged sword of parody, one that "both legitimizes and subverts that which it parodies" (Hutcheon 97), can only be a partial solution to the debilitating "aging as deformation" thesis that prevails throughout popular culture. But even such limited respite proves the *possibility* of alternative discourses, in which the appearance of the aging double, of dissemblance, need not be merely a source of torment. There *are* other options. The difficulty lies not only in seizing them, but first in discerning them.

CONCLUSION

UNCANNY AGING, UNCANNY SELVES

It is true that the statement "All men are mortal" is paraded in text-
books of logic as an example of a general proposition; but no human
being really grasps it, and our unconscious has as little use now as it
ever had for the idea of its own mortality.

    —Freud, "The Uncanny" 364

In the spring the flowers will melt,
also the berries,
and something will come to eat them.
We will go around in these circles for a time,
winter summer winter,
and, after more time, not.

This is a good thought.

    —Margaret Atwood, "Oh"

HOW DOES ONE understand, adapt to, interpret, live with the seeming simultaneous sameness and difference that accompanies old age?
I raised this question in the introduction to this book. In the chapters that
followed I stressed transience and instability, arguing that the continual
transformation resulting from one's status as temporal subject becomes
increasingly apparent, and often problematic, as one ages into old age.
Older subjects often confront, or, perhaps more accurately, *are confronted*
by, the nonfixity and multiplicity of identity at odds with popular fictions
of "true" selves and resilient "cores." I have demonstrated the many forms
such confrontations can take, examining literature and film that explore
uncanny aging in a range of scenarios: the older narrator looking back
on his or her life, caregivers and patients struggling with old age compli-

cated by pathology, subjects facing their own altered image, all situations in which characters confront their own aging, and consequently their own difference.

In her analyses of literary criticism, Barbara Johnson has repeatedly drawn attention to internal inconsistencies that larger patterns of categorization obscure. In *The Critical Difference* Johnson asserts that "[t]he differences *between* entities (prose and poetry, man and woman, literature and theory, guilt and innocence)," and, I would add, young and old, "are shown to be based on a repression of differences *within* entities, ways in which an entity differs from itself" (x–xi). Throughout this book I have proposed that aging into old age strains this repression and triggers unsettling revelations of uncanny identity, of "difference *within*." Some aging studies theorists elide this pervasive and persistent internal difference by restricting uncanniness to later life, interpreting old age as a state that produces a newly divisive subject (for example, Biggs, Hepworth, Holland). Aging theorists have produced a great deal of scholarship on identity in later life, often suggesting that both biological and cultural forces seriously adjust selfhood as subjects enter old age. My own view shifts the site of late-life "newness" from *selfhood* to *self-perception*. Throughout the preceding chapters I have contended that aging into old age does not alter the function or condition of identity itself, but rather, that later life often disrupts our interpretations of subjectivity, dissolving facades of wholeness and stability that obscure the fundamentally unstable human condition. At odds with the fixing effects of popular discourse—the plethora of greeting cards, popular films, jokes, and clichés that enforce polarities of old and young—the aging subject, even the youthful aging subject, is never still, never safely ensconced within a temporal category, since every year, every day, every moment produces alteration. Aging inevitably exposes the illusion of boundaries since the ongoing modification of the subject must inevitably assert itself. As one ages it may become increasingly difficult to distract oneself with overattention to differences between, as difference within becomes undeniably apparent.

Over the course of this book I have offered a widening perspective on uncanny aging, moving from the intimate, internalized realm of (fictional) personal histories and reminiscence to the more public field of specular images. From the first chapter, which concerns processes of reflection and introspection, through the interaction of cognitively impaired subjects and their familial caregivers in the second chapter, to the third chapter's treatment of specular aging, uncanny revelations haunt every scenario. In each of the chapters there is a tension between various, and often conflicting, versions of identity: between those supplied by narrators and their narratives, sufferers and their caregivers, images (reflections, photographs, films) and their human subjects. In these fictional texts, life review, the disruptions of dementia, the glimpse in a mirror, all draw attention to a fundamental mortal instability at odds with impressions of permanence. Despite their different circumstances, the characters in these texts share an altered awareness of identity and time that moves them closer to the recognition of oneself as another. The various conflicts arising from aging into old age in all of these texts reflect a persistent and irresolvable tension between the fluidity of time and characters' staccato-like apprehension of it, which segments time into discrete moments, periods, and ages. The language of aging reflects the problem of shifting versus static identity: the comparative adjective "older" reflects the constancy of aging, and as a result it is a perpetually accurate description of ourselves and others. But the absolutism of the noun "old" enforces the stratification of time and identity, which is arbitrary yet formative. When we are designated "old," or designate ourselves "old," we are fixed and determined by the classification. This temporal categorization, the result of what Woodward calls our "arithmetical" relation to time and aging (*Discontents* 185), produces aging as remarkable and sudden.

So how does one tolerate temporality, that is, an embodied existence subject to constant change that inevitably topples boundaries and categories? Ricoeur suggests that we are protected from the volatility of such mutability by the minute scale of perpetual alteration, by the ability of aging to "threaten resemblance without destroying it" (*Oneself* 117). Throughout the preceding chapters I have examined points of temporal fracture within the hypothetically smooth process of modification, moments when characters suddenly apprehend the changes of aging, perceiving the differences between past and present, young and old selves, that invariably invoke some awareness (however much denied) of the differences *within* the self. My contention is that this awakening to difference carries with it the potential for increased ethical understanding. In the literature and films I have explored, the conflict that arises between competing versions of self provokes a new comprehension of the uncanniness of identity.

SHIFTING FOCUS
Strategies of Response and Resistance

But what does one *do* with such uncanny revelation? In addition to questions concerning identity construction, the introduction raised another, perhaps thornier issue, one regarding strategies of response. Once exposed to our own uncanniness, the unsettling sameness and difference produced by aging, how does one assimilate such an awareness without succumbing to the despair, or even mania, that plague so many of the characters discussed in this book? How does one understand, adapt to, interpret, live with the aftermath of uncanny revelation? In chapter 3 I returned to the issue of response, particularly to *productive* response, concluding my discussion of the "mania of dissemblance" on a hopeful note, suggesting that the comedic parody in *Opening Night* reflects the potential of alternative discourses of aging, strategies of resistance that can undermine, if not always overwrite, the oppressively grim cultural scripts of aging.

Perhaps, as many aging studies scholars suggest, reassigning the cultural meaning of aging into old age is possible, and necessary;[1] however, such a revision would depend, I think, on an altered relationship to temporality, mutability, and strangers, since our antipathy toward aging stems largely from our anxieties surrounding difference and alterity, particularly our own.[2] My own view does not anticipate a change in popular meanings of age as loss and decline, but rather hopes for the cultivation of perspectives that *acknowledge* these bleak associations while promoting alternative interpretations and perceptions. Laughter at the absurdity of aging is common, and although many comedic treatments of old age appear to favor reinforcement rather than resistance, I would hesitate to dismiss ridiculous caricatures, such as Aunt Augusta in Graham Greene's *Travels with My Aunt,* or those played by Jack Lemmon, Walter Matthau, Shirley MacLaine, and others, in a variety of films. Though this conclusion cannot accommodate a prolonged analysis of the various, and often contradictory, functions of comedy, I would like to observe that ridiculous older characters can often upset, if only temporarily, the overattention to youthful heterosexual romance that dominates popular narratives, pointing to

1. Proponents of such revision include Christine Overall, Margaret Morganroth Gullette, Joseph Esposito, and, to a lesser extent, Kathleen Woodward and Stephen Katz.

2. Indeed, the rapidly expanding anti-aging industry effectively divides aging and change, firmly aligning the latter with deficiency. Advertising campaigns for anti-aging products repeatedly claim to have no quarrel with aging itself, but merely with the visual alterations it inflicts. According to popular culture, it is fine to *be* sixty, as long as one does not *look* sixty, a phenomenon Patricia Mellencamp labels "*chronology disavowal*" (286, original emphasis). In discussing the ever-increasing opportunities to "correct" the signs of aging, Mellencamp imagines the amplified marginalization that could result: "Given the uninsured cost of plastic surgery, 'looking old' might become just another disadvantage of being poor" (288).

the continuation of life beyond matchmaking. Such characters often have a trivializing touch, undermining youthful gravity with their absurd perspectives. Though invariably marginalized, older trickster figures and fools provide glimpses of resistant laughter that warrant further investigation.

But as much as laughter and comedic resistance burst through dreary expectations of loss and mourning that accompany narratives of aging, hilarity is difficult to maintain and further tactics prove necessary. Gerontology provides some suggestions. Traditionally, scientific research into aging has tended to focus on deterioration and pathology, but recently there are researchers who counter these dismal trajectories with attention to changes besides loss.[3] Clinical researchers and social scientists have begun to investigate adaptation over time, acknowledging the unavoidability of age-related change without attending exclusively to decline and deterioration. Some gerontological researchers have moved toward a more "multidimensional and multidirectional conception of ageing," one that includes, "besides decline, the possibility of growth or other forms of advance" (Baltes, Freund, and Li 48). This new perspective has produced, among others, the "SOC" theory of aging, which focuses on various age-related changes and the *Substitution, Optimization,* and *Compensation* that result. The SOC theory takes account of *development,* of positive adaptation that can result from the various changes that occur over the lifespan (Baltes, Freund, and Li 54). The shift in focus from changes, in and of themselves, to their *management* introduces researchers to a wide variety of strategies and responses beyond anxiety and distress. Though unsettling strangeness may be undeniable, constructive adaptation is possible.

Likewise, fiction and film addressing the process of aging into old age offer more than narratives of regrettable and unavoidable loss. Without refuting the difficulties of aging, narrative texts often incorporate positive and constructive perspectives on becoming older, depicting characters who nurture the pleasures that persist, and even flourish, over time. Chief among such satisfactions is corporeal pleasure, particularly sexual pleasure. But popular culture often translates late-life sexuality into late-life hedonism, emphasizing the humor of supposedly excessive desire in older subjects. Indeed, comedic "geezer" caricatures often derive much of

3. For a helpful overview of gerontology's increasing attention to the gains of aging, see Ronald J. Manheimer, "Wisdom and Method: Philosophical Contributions to Gerontology." Associations between later life and wisdom are long-standing and the subject of debate in aging studies. See chapter 1 for the details of Erik Erikson's life cycle, which stresses old age as a time of integrity and wisdom.

their humor from their supposedly ridiculous, and even unseemly, desire. Characters such as Aunt Augusta in *Travels with My Aunt*, Maude from Hal Ashby's *Harold and Maude*, Maurice in Roger Michell's *Venus*, or the lecherous old Grandpa Gustafson in Donald Petrie's *Grumpy Old Men* all capitalize on the scandal of sexual desire in old age. "Outrageous" older characters, such as Maude and Maurice, confront their younger counterparts with an affronting sameness—their altered bodies retain desire—that undermines the polarities of sexual youth and neutered old age.[4]

The unabating pleasures of sex not only are the subject of comedic treatments of old age but also frequently appear in serious narratives of aging, often as illicit and disgraceful enactments of desire that contribute to an older character's downfall. In particular, texts exploring the (at least initially) jubilant desire of the old for the young chart the often dangerous repercussions of trespassing generational boundaries. Philip Roth's *The Human Stain*, J. M. Coetzee's *Disgrace*, Doris Lessing's "Grandmothers," along with films such as Roger Michell's *The Mother*, Bill Condon's *Gods and Monsters*, and Richard Eyre's *Notes on a Scandal*, explore sexuality as a continuing source of pleasure and connection for the aging subject, despite the body's changes. But this uncanny persistence of pleasure, at odds with cultural scripts of neutering and diminishment, is commonly transformed into a further site of loss when the "scandalous" affair is finally exposed, the older subject "justifiably" humiliated. Indeed, in each of these texts, "inappropriate" cross-generational desire precipitates some variety of disaster, ranging from loss of employment, to loss of reputation, to loss of life. Relishing the ongoing pleasures of sexuality may be a fulfilling "optimization" of physical ability in later life, but the impropriety of such expressions of vitality proves difficult to escape.[5] If sex between two older characters is typically the source of comedy, sex between older and younger adults often provokes tragedy.

Of course there are exceptions to the pattern. Alice Munro's story "Floating Bridge" concludes with a private expression of desire between an older woman battling cancer, Jinny, and the teenager who escorts her home through a secret shortcut over a floating bridge. The narrative

4. For more on the "metaphoric neutering" of the elderly, see Hockey and James, "Back to Our Futures: Imaging Second Childhood" (145).

5. It is notable that *The Mother*'s protagonist attempts to engage in "appropriate" sexual behavior by subjecting herself to the desires of a man of her own generation. The result is a harrowing scene of sexual violence. For May, a grandmother and widow, any expression of sexuality has serious repercussions, whether with a man her daughter's age or with one her own age.

provides a detailed description of their lingering kiss, an expression of desire that signals the tingling re-emergence of Jinny's hope for survival (her doctor had offered her a new, tentatively optimistic prognosis earlier that day). The story's final lines communicate Jinny's contemplation of her uncanny liminality, both literally—the bridge she stands on hovers between land and water—and more existentially—her shifting diagnosis positions her somewhere between life and death. The transgressive kiss remains private and pleasurable. But the narrator clearly defines the kiss as "the whole story, all by itself" (*Hateship* 82), allowing for an expression of sensuality and kindness without the alarming prospect of transgressive copulation. Indeed, the kiss is more a narrative act than a sexual one, with its "tender prologue," "wholehearted probing and receiving," and "lingering thanks" (82). Kisses between old and young may be productive and permissible, but the pleasures of sex are rarely awarded without complication.

A decidedly less controversial, and subsequently much more common, source of satisfaction for older narrative subjects is the compensatory pleasure of time-earned authority within both the family and the wider community. The trope of the wise elder is far-reaching. The grandparents who appear in novels as diverse as Toni Morrison's *Beloved,* Alistair MacLeod's *No Great Mischief,* and Wayson Choy's *The Jade Peony* are empowered by their life experience. By focusing on the intellectual benefits of a longer life spent learning life lessons, these works portray aging into old age as a process of enlightenment.[6] As well, a selective attention to familial concerns, to the legacy of birth and growth manifested by the appearance of children, grandchildren, and even great-grandchildren, can help compensate for some of the undeniable losses of old age, particularly the illness or disability of the subject or his or her peers (spouses, siblings, friends). Often fiction and film derive much of their emotional resonance by stressing generational continuity, the close bonds between older characters and their children, their children's children, and so on.

Drawing on assumptions of increased familial concerns, later life is often depicted as a time to return to one's "roots,"[7] as though prior to old

6. Texts treating aging as a process of enlightenment echo Erik Erikson's theory of late-life wisdom and "integration," and Lars Tornstam's concept of "gerotranscendence." For an explanation of these developmental models, see Schroots.

7. Alice Munro's collection of stories *The View from Castle Rock* (2006) illustrates this trend in its reimagining of family history. The first part of the collection transforms the lives of Munro's ancestors into short stories, while the second part compiles stories that Munro describes as "closer to my own life than the other stories

age one takes pains to be unencumbered by family and ancestry. David Lynch's film *The Straight Story* illustrates this trend, following seventy-three-year-old Alvin Straight in his painstaking efforts to be reunited with his estranged brother, a compulsion initiated by a new awareness of mortality: Alvin's brother is ill and Alvin himself has recently suffered a stroke. This narrative of late-life reckoning is a story of adaptation in the extreme. Not only does Alvin travel 250 miles despite impairments to his leg and eyes, but he does so on a riding lawn mower since the stroke has deprived him of his driver's license. With minimal dialogue, the film depicts the solemn consolations of old age: silence, solitude, and the natural world.

The film's mise-en-scène literalizes Alvin's expanded perspective in its long shots of landscape, and Alvin himself speaks of the (albeit limited) compensations of becoming older. When a fellow traveler insists, "There must be something good about getting old," Alvin responds, "Well I can't imagine anything good about being blind and lame at the same time, but still at my age I've seen about all that life has to dish out. I know to separate the wheat from the chaff, let the small stuff fall away." In later life Alvin develops an acceptance of, and even appreciation for, that which is incommunicable, even incomprehensible, an expanded perspective reflected in the film's minimal dialogue. Indeed, when he finally reaches his brother, the two exchange few words, and the film concludes with an image of the two old men sitting side-by-side, silently, peacefully enjoying each other's company. As in other films, such as *The Company of Strangers* or Lindsay Anderson's *The Whales of August,* old age functions as a time of quiet companionship or pastoral solitude.[8] In texts such as these, the broadened perspective of later life introduces characters to a new awareness of time's immensity, that is, to nonhuman time, or what one might call natural time. Within the immense scope of natural time, within the enduring cycle of the seasons, one may regard the minute scale of human existence, and even

---

I had written, even in the first person" (*Castle Rock* x). Though not entirely autobiographical, in these stories Munro confessed to be "doing something closer to what memoir does—exploring a life, my own life" (x). In the book's epilogue, Munro explicitly connects aging into old age with the urge to discover one's ancestral past. She explains that old age is a time "when our personal futures close down and we cannot imagine—sometimes cannot believe in—the future of our children's children. We can't resist this rifling around in the past, sifting the untrustworthy evidence, linking stray names and questionable dates and anecdotes together, hanging on to threads, insisting on being joined to dead people and therefore to life" (347).

8. This perspective on aging risks slipping into a stereotypical vision of old age as a time when inaction dominates, when "being" overtakes "doing." Though this dichotomy has obvious disadvantages, there are benefits to emphasizing the quiet, inner activity of later life, as Woodward makes clear in her reflections on the "*pleasures of inactivity*" in older age (*Discontents* 179, original emphasis).

find comfort in one's small participation in the continuity of nature, as in the epigraph to this conclusion from Margaret Atwood. Such an expansive perspective can advance the concerns of multigenerational narratives, allowing for the integration of change and continuity; the family goes on and on, one generation replacing another, presenting the pleasing illusion of perpetuity.

The impossibility of apprehending the minute, ongoing actions of aging means that aging, though constant, often seems to occur suddenly, producing numerous problems for subjectivity and identity, as the previous chapters demonstrate. The underlying temporality of identity results in an uncanny condition that can be difficult to abide since it resists complete comprehension, being always in a process of development. As a result, epistemological traditions accustomed to respecting, and even embracing, incomprehensibility may be well equipped to contend with the uncanniness of aging. In Marilynne Robinson's novel *Gilead,* the narrator, Reverend John Ames, contemplates the strangeness of his own mortality and the strangeness of divinity with similar awe and resignation. For John Ames, in his mid-seventies, the mystery of mortal existence is both confounding and beautiful, and he looks back at his life (not without an element of sadness and regret) and forward to his own death with a tolerance for its incomprehensibility rarely found in the narratives explored in my previous chapters. Moments of reminiscence, which allow him to be at once in the present and in the past, provoke "sweetness in the experience which I don't understand. But that only enhances the value of it. My point here is that you never do know the actual nature even of your own experience. Or perhaps that it has no fixed and certain nature" (95). In *Gilead,* Christian spirituality assists the narrator in embracing the incomprehensibility, and even the absurdity, of human temporality, of mortality. As a result, *Gilead* offers a moving portrait of age, one that examines uncanny mutability without collapsing into despair or mania.

Ames's narrative of reminiscence eschews narrative totality by incorporating spirituality and addressing profundity and irresolution directly without the goal of comprehension or clear conclusions. He embraces the grand mystery of earthly existence and at the same time attends to the concrete details of the everyday. The novel raises the possibility of perceiving the constitutive instability of selfhood without crisis. Ames's trust in divinity heightens both his awareness and his accommodation of the strangeness and mysteriousness of existence.[9] *Gilead* is a compelling response to

9. The closest secular approximation of Ames's perspective might be found in *The Company of Strangers,* which includes contemplative scenes of wordless "being" and reminiscence that do not serve a larger teleological project.

Johnson's criticism of the problematic overattention to differences *between* entities in order to shroud those more difficult, even alarming, differences *within*. For John Ames, the revelations of his own strangeness brought on by age are confirmations of a larger mystery that couples all his regrets over temporal changes with awe at the movements of life. Aging teaches Ames to understand the limits of his own understanding:

> People talk about how wonderful the world seems to children, and that's true enough. But children think they will grow into it and understand it, and I know very well that I will not, and would not if I had a dozen lives. That's clearer to me every day. Each morning I'm like Adam waking up in Eden, amazed at the cleverness of my hands and at the brilliance pouring into my mind through my eyes—old hands, old eyes, old mind, a very diminished Adam altogether, and still it is just remarkable. (66)

In *Gilead* readers discover a narrator who not only *tolerates* mystery and strangeness within but respects and even loves the incomprehensible since for him it is an element of grace.

For the narrating Reverend, the Christian tradition provides a means for approaching and appreciating the mysteriousness of existence, both his own and others', a perspective that recalls Levinas's theories of alterity and responsibility, which emphasize the subject's fundamental obligation to the other (as discussed in chapter 2). Levinas is not alone in emphasizing obligation as primary to humanity, though not all moral philosophers cast responsibility in such terms. There is a substantial body of criticism that regards care as a fundamental human need, privileging caring relations as primary, sustaining, and fulfilling. Theorists of the ethics of care, such as Virginia Held, Eva Kittay, Carol Gilligan, and Maurice Hamington, stress that life itself is founded upon caring human relations, insisting that identity is first and foremost relational and dependent: "[t]he fact of human vulnerability and frailty that dependency underscores must function in our very conception of ourselves as subjects and moral agents" (Kittay and Feder 3). The burdensome obligation that Levinas describes is recast as the source of humanity and meaning. Held describes "persons as embedded and encumbered" (15), drawing on Gilligan's explication of the "paradoxical truths of human experience—that we know ourselves as separate only insofar as we live in connection with others, and that we experience relationships only insofar as we differentiate other from self" (Gilligan 63). As Held, Gilligan, and others point out, such "encumbered-ness" is too easily overlooked or dismissed in a culture that privileges independence and individuality. The illness and disability that often accompany aging into old age upend illusions of autonomous identity, of persons as discrete, independent, and comprehendible. According to philosopher Kelly Oliver, dependence and independence are paradoxically entwined, each one producing the other:

> [O]ne's own independence requires acknowledging one's indebtedness to the world and others. . . . [T]his dependent foundation of subjectivity brings with it an ethical obligation to the world and others. Dependence is not a sign of a lack of freedom or a lack of agency; and independence is not total disconnection from others and the earth. Insofar as subjectivity is produced in, and sustained by, our relation to the world and others, an ethical obligation lies at the heart of subjectivity itself. ("Subjectivity" 324–25)

For Oliver, "subjectivity and humanity" depend on what she calls "response-ability," that is, "the ability to respond and be responded to" (*Witnessing* 91). The transformation of "responsibility" into "response-ability" enables a "double sense" of both "opening up the ability to respond—response-ability—and ethically obligating subjects to respond by virtue of their very subjectivity itself" (91). For ethics of care theorists, obligation to and dependence on others is neither unusual nor temporary, but is a predictable and necessary aspect of human existence. With "encumbered-ness" comes "embeddedness," that is, with burdensome responsibility come the human relationships essential for life and meaning.

The inevitability of dependence and responsibility, often exposed by aging into old age, can force subjects to confront uncanny identity and their obligation "to respond to what is beyond . . . comprehension, beyond recognition, because ethics is possible only beyond recognition" (Oliver 106). John Ames's profoundest apprehension of the wondrous incomprehensibility of mortality comes in expressions of love for others, both in formal bestowals of blessings and in private interactions and exchanges with family and friends. His respect for both the alterity of the other and the alterity of the self produces a variety of ethical dilemmas in which he must examine the hierarchy of his commitments, choosing whether to prioritize forgiveness or protection, family or others, contemplation or action. The ethical predicaments that arise out of Ames's efforts to respect and cherish the mystery of identity, both the self's and the other's, expose the fundamental importance and ethical complexity of expressions of care. In Robinson's novel, aging into old age involves an increasing admiration for the mysteriousness of the other, as well as the innate mysteriousness of the self, demonstrating the immense power of what is commonly called love. But just as *Gilead* glorifies the incomprehensibility of the human subject and its relations, it also shows the difficulty of "appropriately" responding to such glorious, incomprehensible others.

With its exposure of the uncanniness of identity and potential to awaken the subject to the mystery of others, aging into old age can provoke a new appreciation for human connections, as seen in the narratives of aging that celebrate family connections, ancestry, and generational continuity (Choy, MacLeod, Munro, Robinson). As one ages into extreme old age, late-life illness and disability often increase dependence on others. For such subjects, contemplating "care" is far from a sentimental or frivolous pursuit since its expressions are increasingly linked to comfort and even survival. The centrality of care returns me to earlier questions of survival. How does one live with the simultaneous sameness and difference that emerges in old age? Perhaps the most promising and probable answer is "with assistance." The operations of identity and responsibility explored throughout this book, particularly in chapter 2, lead me to believe that the meaning and function of "care" are fundamental to discussions of subjectivity and alterity, not only as one ages into old age, but throughout the life course. Relationality is central to the condition of identity, and the human interaction that occurs in caregiving confirms the fundamental importance of dependence and responsibility in discussions of selfhood.

In chapter 1, I referred to Barthes's oft-cited correlation of aging and photographic representation as twin producers of disincarnation. The assessment of aging as "disincarnation" says as much about the means of apprehension as it does about aging itself. Perceived through cultural lenses and frames that, much like the photograph, arrest the fluidity of human temporality, segmenting the life course and the population into dualistic categories of old and young, "over the hill" or still approaching it, aging may indeed appear as a process of dissemblance and disintegration. However, it is possible, if only occasionally, to perceive the uncanniness of our continuous alteration. Tolerating, and even appreciating, one's own aging, with all its ensuing strangeness, absurdity, and indecipherability, can be a profoundly political act since, by recognizing this strangeness within, one may find a new tolerance for the strangeness of others. As such, the uncanniness of aging can affirm that "strangers are both *within* us and *beyond* us" (Kearney, *Strangers* 229, original emphasis), leading us closer to a productive space of respect and dialogue. As Kearney insists, "strangeness need not always estrange us to the point of dehumanisation"

(231); that which is beyond the limits of human comprehension need not provoke only anxiety and despair. With echoes of Levinas, Robinson's character John Ames proposes that the face of the other is a "vision" that can provoke a "mystical" awareness of incarnation, and its corresponding responsibilities: "in my present situation, now that I am about to leave this world, I realize there is nothing more astonishing than a human face. . . . It has something to do with incarnation. You feel your obligation to a child when you have seen it and held it. Any human face is a claim on you, because you can't help but understand the singularity of it, the courage and loneliness of it" (66). If aging is at least partly a process of disincarnation, contact with the other can return us to the space of incarnation, transferring our attention away from diminishing capabilities to the enduring mystery of identity and existence, both within and without.

ENDINGS

Discussions of aging are always obliquely discussions of mortality. The same might be said of the uncanny. The prospect of such an absolute conclusion is so unthinkable as to demand strenuous, ongoing repression, as the epigraph from Freud that opens this conclusion indicates. The mortal condition is unavoidably uncanny: though death is our guaranteed conclusion, it remains unknown and incomprehensible. For all of Freud's efforts to expose our repression of our own inevitable ending, his literary endings are notoriously indirect and diverting. "The Uncanny" concludes with a rather arresting redirection. Directly after elucidating some of the differences between the effects of certain uncanny events and their literary representations, Freud ends his essay with a brief paragraph: "Concerning the factors of silence, solitude and darkness we can say only that they are actually elements in the production of the infantile anxiety from which the majority of human beings have never become quite free. This problem has been discussed from a psychoanalytic point of view elsewhere" (376). This startling change of subject substitutes diversion for summary, drawing attention to the essay's own lack of explanation, thereby reinstating uncanniness.

In "The Uncanny," Freud delves into various "primitive" and infantile anxieties that have been buried over time only to be unearthed by some sight or sound that consequently becomes uncanny, but he repeatedly shuttles these "factors" ("silence, solitude and darkness") to the periphery of his discussion (376, 369). According to Freud, silence, solitude, and darkness are unrelentingly distressing, their power to unsettle never overcome by maturation. Often aging into old age returns these anxiety-provoking "factors" to the forefront of daily experience, but communication, company, and illumination can counter their effect. The frequent necessity of assistance in later life emphasizes the relationality of subjectivity, forcing one to reckon with both one's debt to, and responsibility for, the other. Denying the difficulties of aging, whether increased silence and solitude, illness or disability, or awareness of darkness and death, is counterproductive. Seizing new possibilities, perceptions, and relations that arise from perpetual modification can relieve, or least mitigate, some of these disabilities. The "biological facts" that guarantee the "dreaded decline" Beauvoir laments (46) are only one part of the story of aging. Narrative fiction and film remind us of our own narrativity, our uncanny condition as perpetually "in progress," and both the fragility and possibility such instability ensures.

WORKS CITED

Abbott, Porter. *The Cambridge Introduction to Narrative*. New York: Cambridge University Press, 2002.

———. "The Future of All Narrative Futures." In *A Companion to Narrative Theory*, edited by James Phelan and Peter Rabinowitz. Malden, MA: Blackwell, 2005. 529–41.

"About the Institute." Buck Institute. 8 July 2007. http://www.buckinstitute.org/site/index.php?option=com_content&task=view&id=262&Itemid=320.

Achenbaum, W. Andrew. "Ageing and Changing: International Historical Perspectives on Ageing." In *The Cambridge Handbook of Age and Ageing*, 21–29.

Adderson, Caroline. *A History of Forgetting*. Toronto: Patrick Crean Editions, 1999.

All About Eve. Directed by Joseph L. Mankiewicz. Performed by Anne Baxter, Bette Davis. 20th Century Fox Home Entertainment, 1950.

Baltes, Paul, Alexandra Freund, and Schu-Chen Li. "The Psychological Science of Human Ageing." In *The Cambridge Handbook of Age and Ageing*, 47–71.

Banville, John. *Shroud*. London: Picador, 2002.

Barthes, Roland. *Camera Lucida: Reflections on Photography*. Translated by Richard Howard. New York: Hill and Wang, 1981.

———. *Image, Music, Text*. Translated by Stephen Heath. New York: Hill and Wang, 1978.

Baum, Rosalie Murphy. "Self-Alienation of the Elderly in Margaret Laurence's Fiction." In *New Perspectives on Margaret Laurence*, 153–60.

Bayley, John. *Elegy for Iris*. New York: St. Martin's, 1999.

———. *Iris: A Memoir of Iris Murdoch*. London: Duckworth, 1998.

Beauvoir, Simone de. *Old Age.* Translated by Patrick O'Brian. Harmondsworth, UK: Penguin, 1977.

Bell, Alice. "Hagar Shipley's Rage for Life: Narrative Technique in *The Stone Angel.*" In *New Perspectives on Margaret Laurence,* 51–62.

Berliner, Todd. "Hollywood Movie Dialogue and the 'Real Realism' of John Cassavetes." *Film Quarterly* 52, no. 3 (1999): 2–16.

Biggs, Simon. "The 'Blurring' of the Lifecourse: Narrative, Memory and the Question of Authenticity." *Journal of Aging and Identity* 4, no. 4 (1999): 209–21.

———. *The Mature Imagination: Dynamics of Identity in Midlife and Beyond.* Philadelphia: Open University Press, 1999.

Blau, Herbert. "The Makeup of Memory in the Winter of Our Discontent." In Schwartz and Woodward, *Memory and Desire,* 13–36.

Bordwell, David, and Kristen Thompson. *Film Art: An Introduction.* 5th ed. New York: McGraw-Hill, 1997.

Bowden, Peta. "Theoretical Care: Feminism, Theory and Ethics." *Critical Review* 33 (1993): 129–47.

Bronfen, Elisabeth. "The Death Drive (Freud)." In *Feminism and Psychoanalysis: A Critical Dictionary,* edited by Elizabeth Wright. Cambridge, MA, and Oxford: Blackwell, 1992. 52–57.

Brooks, Jodi. "Performing Aging/Performance Crisis (for Norma Desmond, Baby-Jane, Margo Channing, Sister George—and Myrtle)." In Woodward, *Figuring Age,* 232–47.

Butler, Robert. "The Life Review: An Interpretation of Reminiscence in the Aged." *Psychiatry* 26 (1963): 65–76.

Butte, George. *I Know That You Know That I Know: Narrating Subjects from Moll Flanders to Marnie.* Columbus: The Ohio State University Press, 2004.

The Cambridge Handbook of Age and Ageing. Edited by Malcolm L. Johnson. Cambridge: Cambridge University Press, 2005.

Carney, Raymond. *The Films of John Cassavetes: Pragmatism, Modernism, and the Movies.* New York: Cambridge University Press, 1994.

Carth, Cathy, ed. *Trauma: Explorations in Memory.* Baltimore: Johns Hopkins University Press, 1995.

Caruth, Cathy. Introduction to *Trauma: Explorations in Memory,* edited by Cathy Caruth. Baltimore: Johns Hopkins University Press, 1995. 3–12.

———. *Unclaimed Experience: Trauma, Narrative, and History.* Baltimore: Johns Hopkins University Press, 1996.

Cassel, Christine K. Foreword to *Ethical Foundations of Palliative Care for Alzheimer Disease,* edited by Ruth B. Purtilo. Baltimore and London: Johns Hopkins University Press, 2004. ix–xi.

Chivers, Sally. *From Old Woman to Older Women: Contemporary Culture and Women's Narratives.* Columbus: The Ohio State University Press, 2003.

Choy, Wayson. *The Jade Peony.* Vancouver, BC: Douglas & McIntyre, 1995.

Cixous, Hélène. "Fiction and Its Fantoms: A Reading of Freud's Das Unheimliche (the 'Uncanny')." *New Literary History* 7, no. 3 (1976): 525–48.

Coetzee, J. M. *Disgrace.* London: Vintage, 2000.

Cohen, Elizabeth. *The House on Beartown Road: A Memoir of Learning and Forgetting.* London: Vermilion, 2004.

Comeau, Paul. "Hagar in Hell: Margaret Laurence's Fallen Angel." *Canadian Literature* 128 (1991): 11–22.

The Company of Strangers. Directed by Cynthia Scott. National Film Board, 1990.

Creed, Barbara. *The Monstrous-Feminine: Film, Feminism, Psychoanalysis.* New York: Routledge, 1993.

Culler, Jonathan D. *The Pursuit of Signs: Semiotics, Literature, Deconstruction.* Ithaca, NY: Cornell University Press, 1981.

The Cultural Studies Reader. 2nd ed. Edited by Simon During. London and New York: Routledge, 1999.

Davis, Robert. *My Journey into Alzheimer's Disease.* Edited by Betty Davis. Wheaton, IL: Tyndale House, 1989.

De Man, Paul. *Allegories of Reading: Figural Language in Rousseau, Nietzsche, Rilke, and Proust.* New Haven, CT: Yale University Press, 1979.

Demos, John. "Old Age in Early New England." In Van Tassel, *Aging, Death, and the Completion of Being,* 115–64.

DeBaggio, Thomas. *Losing My Mind: An Intimate Look at Life with Alzheimer's.* London: Free Press, 2002.

D'hoker, Elke. *Visions of Alterity: Representation in the Works of John Banville.* Amsterdam: Rodopi, 2004.

Doane, Mary Ann. *Femmes Fatales: Feminism, Film Theory, Psychoanalysis.* New York: Routledge, 1991.

Dyer, Richard. *Heavenly Bodies: Film Stars and Society.* New York: St. Martin's, 1986.

Eakin, Paul John. *How Our Lives Become Stories: Making Selves.* Ithaca, NY: Cornell University Press, 1999.

———. "Introduction: Mapping the Ethics of Life Writing." In *The Ethics of Life Writing,* edited by Paul John Eakin. Ithaca, NY: Cornell University Press, 2004. 1–16.

———. "What Are We Reading When We Read Autobiography?" *Narrative* 12, no. 2 (2004): 121–32.

"Editor's note to all women over 60." Editorial Response. *More* (Summer 2007): 18.

Erikson, Erik H. *The Life Cycle Completed.* Edited by Joan M. Erikson. New York: W. W. Norton, 1997.

Esposito, Joseph L. *The Obsolete Self: Philosophical Dimensions of Aging.* Berkeley: University of California Press, 1987.

Fabre, Michel, Marie Bell-Salter, and Raymonde Neil. "The Angel and the Living Water: Metaphorical Networks and Structural Opposition in *The Stone Angel.*" In *New Perspectives on Margaret Laurence,* 17–28.

"Fact Sheet: Alzheimer's Disease Statistics." Alzheimer's Association. 14 April 2006. http://www.alz.org/Resources/FactSheets/FSAlzheimerStats.pdf.

Featherstone, Mike, and Andrew Wernick. Introduction to Featherstone and Wernick, *Images of Aging,* 1–15.

———, eds. *Images of Aging: Cultural Representations of Later Life.* London: Routledge, 1995.

Felman, Shoshana, and Dori Laub. *Testimony: Crises of Witnessing in Literature, Psychoanalysis, and History.* New York: Routledge, 1992.

Fortunati, Vita. *The Controversial Women's Body: Images and Representations in Literature and Art.* Bologna: Bononia University Press, 2003.

Franzen, Jonathan. *The Corrections.* Toronto: HarperCollins, 2001.

———. *How to Be Alone.* London: Harper Perennial, 2004.

Freud, Sigmund. "Fetishism." In *On Sexuality: Three Essays on the Theory of Sexuality and Other Works,* translated by James Strachey, edited by James Strachey and Angela Richards. London: Penguin, 1977. 345–57.

———. "'The 'Uncanny.'" In *Art and Literature,* translated by James Strachey, edited by James Strachey and Angela Richards. London: Penguin, 1985. 335–76.

Garland, Jeff, and Christina Garland. *Life Review in Health and Social Care: A Practitioner's Guide.* Philadelphia: Brunner-Routledge, 2001.

Garrison, William Lloyd. Preface to *Narrative of the Life of Frederick Douglass, an American Slave,* by Frederick Douglass. 1845. New York: Penguin, 1986. 33–42.

George, Diana Hume. "Who Is the Double Ghost Whose Head Is Smoke?: Women Poets on Aging." In Schwartz and Woodward, *Memory and Desire,* 134–53.

Gilligan, Carol. *In a Different Voice: Psychological Theory and Women's Development.* Cambridge: Harvard University Press, 1982.

Gods and Monsters. Directed by Bill Condon. Performed by Brendan Fraser, Ian McKellen. Lions Gate Home Entertainment, 1998.

Grant, Linda. *Remind Me Who I Am Again.* London: Granta, 1998.

Greene, Graham. *Travels with My Aunt.* Harmondsworth, UK: Penguin, 1971.

Grumpy Old Men. Directed by Donald Petrie. Performed by Jack Lemmon, Walter Matthau. Warner Brothers, 1993.

Gullette, Margaret Morganroth. *Aged by Culture.* Chicago: University of Chicago Press, 2004.

———. *Declining to Decline: Cultural Combat and the Politics of the Midlife.* Charlottesville, VA: University Press of Virginia, 1997.

———. "The Other End of the Fashion Cycle: Practicing Loss, Learning Decline." In Woodward, *Figuring Age,* 34–55.

———. *Safe at Last in the Middle Years, the Invention of the Midlife Progress Novel: Saul Bellow, Margaret Drabble, Anne Tyler, and John Updike.* Berkeley: University of California Press, 1988.

Gunning, Tom. "Phantom Images and Modern Manifestations: Spirit Photography, Magic Theater, Trick Films, and Photography's Uncanny." In *Fugitive Images: From Photography to Film,* edited by Patrice Petro. Bloomington: Indiana University Press, 1995. 42–71.

Hamington, Maurice. *Embodied Care: Jane Addams, Maurice Merleau-Ponty, and Feminist Ethics.* Urbana and Chicago: University of Illinois Press, 2004.

Harold and Maude. Directed by Hal Ashby. Performed by Bud Cort, Ruth Gordon. Paramount Home Video, 1971.

Hartman, Geoffrey. *The Longest Shadow: In the Aftermath of the Holocaust.* New York: Palgrave Macmillan, 2002.

Haskell, Molly. *From Reverence to Rape: The Treatment of Women in the Movies.* New York: Holt, 1975.

Hazan, Haim. *Old Age: Constructions and Deconstructions*. New York: Cambridge University Press, 1994.

Heble, Ajay. *The Tumble of Reason: Alice Munro's Discourse of Absence*. Toronto: University of Toronto Press, 1994.

Held, Virginia. *The Ethics of Care*. Oxford: Oxford University Press, 2006.

Hemmings, Robert. "'The Blameless Physician': Narrative and Pain, Sassoon and Rivers." *Literature and Medicine* 24, no. 1 (2005): 109–26.

Hepworth, Mike. *Stories of Ageing*. Philadelphia: Open University Press, 2000.

Hockey, Jenny, and Allison James. "Back to Our Futures: Imaging Second Childhood." In Featherstone and Wernick, *Images of Aging*, 135–48.

Holland, Norman. "Not So Little Hans: Identity and Aging." In Schwartz and Woodward, *Memory and Desire*, 51–75.

Holmes, Richard. "The Proper Study?" In *Mapping Lives: The Uses of Biography*, edited by Peter France and William St. Clair. Oxford: Oxford University Press, 2002. 7–18.

Howells, Coral Ann. *Alice Munro*. New York: Manchester University Press, 1998.

———. *Contemporary Canadian Women's Fiction: Refiguring Identities*. New York: Palgrave Macmillan, 2003.

Husserl, Edmund. *The Crisis of European Sciences and Transcendental Phenomenology: An Introduction to Phenomenological Philosophy*. Evanston, IL: Northwestern University Press, 1970.

Hutcheon, Linda. *The Politics of Postmodernism*. New York: Routledge, 1991.

Identities: Race, Class, Gender and Nationality. Edited by Linda Alcoff and Eduardo Mendieta. Malden, MA: Blackwell, 2003.

Imhof, Rüdiger. "'The Problematics of Authenticity': John Banville's *Shroud*." *ABEI Journal: The Brazilian Journal of Irish Studies* 6 (2004): 105–27.

Iris. Directed by Richard Eyre. Performed by Hugh Bonneville, Jim Broadbent, Judi Dench, Kate Winslet. Miramax Films, 2001.

Jameson, Fredric. *The Political Unconscious: Narrative as a Socially Symbolic Act*. London: Routledge, 2002.

Jamieson, Sara. "The Fiction of Agelessness: Work, Leisure, and Aging in Alice Munro's 'Pictures of the Ice.'" *Studies in Canadian Literature/Études en Littérature Canadienne* 29, no. 1 (2004): 106–26.

Johnson, Barbara. *The Critical Difference: Essays in the Contemporary Rhetoric of Reading*. Baltimore: Johns Hopkins University Press, 1980.

———. *The Feminist Difference: Literature, Psychoanalysis, Race, and Gender*. Cambridge, MA: Harvard University Press, 1998.

Kaplan, E. Ann. "Trauma, Aging, and Melodrama." In *Feminist Locations: Global and Local, Theory and Practice*, edited by Marianne Dekoven. New Brunswick, NJ: Rutgers University Press, 2001. 304–28.

———. "Trauma and Aging: Marlene Dietrich, Melanie Klein, and Marguerite Duras." In Woodward, *Figuring Age*, 171–94.

———. "Wicked Old Ladies from Europe: Jeanne Moreau and Marlene Dietrich on the Screen and Live." In *Bad: Infamy, Darkness, Evil, and Slime on Screen*, edited by Murray Pomerance. Albany: State University of New York Press, 2004. 239–53.

Kaplan, David M. *Ricoeur's Critical Theory*. Albany: State University of New York Press, 2003.

Katz, Steven. *Disciplining Old Age: The Formation of Gerontological Knowledge*. Charlottesville: University Press of Virginia, 1996.

———. "Imagining the Life-Span: From Premodern Miracles to Postmodern Fantasies." In Featherstone and Wernick, *Images of Aging*, 61–75.

Kaufman, Sharon R. *The Ageless Self: Sources of Meaning in Late Life*. Madison: University of Wisconsin Press, 1986.

Kausler, Barry C., and Donald H. Kausler. *The Graying of America: An Encyclopedia of Aging, Health, Mind, and Behavior*. 2nd ed. Urbana: University of Illinois Press, 2001.

Kearney, Richard. *On Stories*. New York: Routledge, 2002.

———. *Strangers, Gods, and Monsters: Ideas of Otherness*. New York: Routledge, 2003.

Kenyon, Gary M., and William Lowell Randall. *Restorying Our Lives: Personal Growth Through Autobiographical Reflection*. Westport, CT: Praeger, 1997.

Kerby, Anthony Paul. *Narrative and the Self*. Bloomington: Indiana University Press, 1991.

King, Homay. "Free Indirect Affect in Cassavetes' *Opening Night* and *Faces*." *Camera Obscura* 19, no. 2 (2004): 105–39.

Kittay, Eva Feder. *Love's Labor: Essays on Women, Equality, and Dependency*. London: Routledge, 1999.

Kittay, Eva Feder, and Ellen K. Feder. Introduction to Kittay and Feder, *The Subject of Care*, 1–12.

———, eds. *The Subject of Care: Feminist Perspectives on Dependency*. New York: Rowman and Littlefield, 2002.

Kittler, Friedrich. "Romanticism—Psychoanalysis—Film: A History of the Double." In *Literature, Media, Information Systems*, edited by John Johnston. Amsterdam: G+B Arts International, 1975. 85–100.

Koestenbaum, Wayne. *Double Talk: The Erotics of Male Literary Collaboration*. New York: Routledge, 1989.

Kofman, Sarah. *Freud and Other Fictions*, translated by Sarah Wykes. Cambridge: Polity, 1991.

Kondratowitz, Hans-Joachim von. "The Medicalization of Old Age: Continuity and Change in Germany from the Late Eighteenth to the Early Twentieth Century." In *Life, Death, and the Elderly: Historical Perspectives*, edited by Margaret Pelling and Richard M. Smith. London: Routledge, 1991. 134–64.

Kristeva, Julia. *Powers of Horror: An Essay on Abjection*. Translated by Leon S. Roudiez. New York: Columbia University Press, 1982.

———. *Strangers to Ourselves*. Translated by Leon S. Roudiez. New York: Columbia University Press, 1991.

Krystal, Henry. "Trauma and Aging: A Thirty-Year Follow-Up." In *Trauma: Explorations in Memory*, edited by Cathy Caruth. Baltimore: Johns Hopkins University Press, 1995. 76–99.

Kuhn, Annette. *Family Secrets: Acts of Memory and Imagination*. New York: Verso, 2002.

LaCapra, Dominick. *Writing History, Writing Trauma*. Baltimore: Johns Hopkins University Press, 2001.

Laslett, Peter. "The Traditional English Family and the Aged in Our Society." In Van Tassel, *Aging, Death, and the Completion of Being*, 97–114.

Laub, Dori. "Truth and Testimony: The Process and the Struggle." In *Trauma: Explorations in Memory*, edited by Cathy Caruth. Baltimore, MD: Johns Hopkins University Press, 1995. 61–75.

Laurence, Margaret. *The Stone Angel*. Toronto: McClelland and Stewart, 1988.

Lessing, Doris May. *The Grandmothers: Four Short Novels*. New York: Perennial, 2005.

Levinas, Emmanuel. *Otherwise Than Being: Or, Beyond Essence*. Translated by Alphonso Lingis. Boston: Kluwer, 1991.

Levinas, Emmanuel, and Richard Kearney. "Dialogue with Emmanuel Levinas." In *Face to Face with Levinas*, edited by Richard A. Cohen. Albany: State University of New York Press, 1986. 3–34.

Levine, Judith. *Do You Remember Me?: A Father, a Daughter, and a Search for the Self*. New York: Free Press, 2004.

Lindesay, James, Kenneth Rockwood, and Daryl Rolfson. "The Epidemiology of Delirium." In *Ethical Foundations of Palliative Care for Alzheimer Disease*, edited by Ruth B. Purtilo. Baltimore and London: Johns Hopkins University Press, 2004. 27–50.

Lloyd Smith, Allan. *Uncanny American Fiction: Medusa's Face*. New York: St. Martin's, 1989.

Lothe, Jakob. *Narrative in Fiction and Film: An Introduction*. New York: Oxford University Press, 2000.

Luborsky, Mark. "Creative Challenges and the Construction of Meaningful Life Narratives." In *Creativity and Successful Aging: Theoretical and Empirical Approaches*, edited by Carolyn E. Adams-Price. New York: Springer, 1998. 311–37.

Lydenberg, Robin. "Freud's Uncanny Narratives." *PMLA* 112, no. 5 (1997): 1072–86.

MacIntyre, Alasdair C. *After Virtue: A Study in Moral Theory*. 2nd ed. Notre Dame, IN: University of Notre Dame Press, 1984.

MacLeod, Alistair. *No Great Mischief*. Toronto: Emblem Editions, 2001.

Mangum, Teresa. "Little Women: The Aging Female Character in Nineteenth-Century British Children's Literature" In Woodward, *Figuring Age*, 59–87.

Manheimer, Ronald J. "Wisdom and Method: Philosophical Contributions to Gerontology." In *Handbook of the Humanities and Aging*, edited by Thomas R. Cole, David D. Van Tassel, and Robert Kastenbaum. New York: Springer, 1992. 426–40.

Marcus, Steven. "Freud and Dora: Story, History, Case History." In *In Dora's Case*, edited by Charles Bernheimer and Claire Kahane. New York: Columbia University Press, 1985. 56–91.

McLeish, John A. B. *The Ulyssean Adult: Creativity in the Middle and Later Years*. New York: McGraw-Hill Ryerson, 1976.

Meigs, Mary. "On Aging." *Canadian Woman Studies/Les Cahiers de la Femme* 5, no. 3 (1984): 67–69.

Mellencamp, Patricia. *High Anxiety: Catastrophe, Scandal, Age and Comedy.* Bloomington: Indiana University Press, 1992.

Miller, Sue. *The Story of My Father: A Memoir.* New York: Knopf, 2003.

Mitchell, Marilyn. *Dancing on Quicksand: A Gift of Friendship in the Age of Alzheimer's* Boulder, CO: Johnson, 2002.

Mooney, Linda A., David Knox, and Caroline Schacht. *Understanding Social Problems.* 2nd ed. Belmont, CA: Wadsworth, 2000.

Moore, Jeffrey S. *The Memory Artists.* Toronto: Viking Canada, 2004.

Morgenstern, Naomi. "The Baby or the Violin? Ethics and Femininity in the Fiction of Alice Munro." *LIT: Literature Interpretation Theory* 14, no. 2 (2003): 69–97.

Morrison, Toni. *Beloved.* New York: Penguin Books, 2000.

The Mother. Directed by Roger Michell. Performed by Daniel Craig, Anne Reid. Sony Pictures Classics, 2003.

Mulvey, Laura. "Visual Pleasure and Narrative Cinema." In *Issues in Feminist Film Criticism,* edited by Patricia Erens. Bloomington and Indianapolis: Indiana University Press, 1990. 28–40.

Munro, Alice. *Hateship, Friendship, Courtship, Loveship, Marriage.* Toronto: McClelland and Stewart, 2001.

———. *Lives of Girls and Women.* Toronto: Penguin Canada, 2005.

———. *Runaway.* Toronto: McClelland and Stewart, 2004.

———. *The View from Castle Rock.* Toronto: McClelland and Stewart, 2006.

———. *Who Do You Think You Are?* Toronto: Penguin, 1996.

New Perspectives on Margaret Laurence: Poetic Narrative, Multiculturalism, and Feminism. Edited by Greta M. K. McCormick Coger. Westport, CT: Greenwood, 1996.

The Notebook. Directed by Nick Cassavetes. Performed by Gena Rowlands, James Garner, Rachel McAdams, Ryan Gosling. Alliance Atlantis Home Video, 2004.

Notes on a Scandal. Directed by Richard Eyre. Performed by Judi Dench, Kate Blanchett. Fox Searchlight Pictures, 2006.

Oliver, Kelly. "Subjectivity as Responsivity: The Ethical Implications of Dependency." In Kittay and Feder, *The Subject of Care,* 322–33.

———. *Witnessing: Beyond Recognition.* Minneapolis: University of Minnesota Press, 2001.

Olson, Laura Katz, ed. *The Graying of the World: Who Will Care for the Frail Elderly?* New York: Haworth, 1994.

Opening Night. Directed by John Cassavetes. Performed by Joan Blondell, John Cassavetes, Ben Gazzara, Gena Rowlands. Faces Distributing, 1977.

Overall, Christine. *Aging, Death, and Human Longevity: A Philosophical Inquiry.* Berkeley: University of California Press, 2003.

Page, P. K. *A Kind of Fiction.* Erin, ON: Porcupine's Quill, 2001.

Pennee, Donna Palmateer. "Technologies of Identity: The Language of the Incontinent Body in Margaret Laurence's *The Stone Angel.*" *Studies in Canadian Literature/Études en Littérature Canadienne* 25, no. 2 (2000): 1–23.

Peperzak, Adriaan Theodoor. *Beyond: The Philosophy of Emmanuel Levinas.* Evanston, IL: Northwestern University Press, 1997.

Phelan, James. "Who's Here? Thoughts on Narrative Identity and Narrative Imperialism." *Narrative* 13, no. 3 (2005): 205–10.

Purtilo, Ruth B., ed. *Ethical Foundations of Palliative Care for Alzheimer Disease.* Baltimore and London: Johns Hopkins University Press, 2004.

Rank, Otto. *Beyond Psychology.* Edited by Northrop Frye. New York: Dover, 1958.

———. *The Double: A Psychoanalytic Study.* Chapel Hill: University of North Carolina Press, 1971.

Redekop, Magdalene. *Mothers and Other Clowns: The Stories of Alice Munro.* New York: Routledge, 1992.

Requiem for a Dream. Directed by Darren Aronofsky. Performed by Ellen Burstyn, Jared Leto, Jennifer Connelly. Lions Gate Films, 2000.

Richler, Mordecai. *Barney's Version.* New York: Knopf, 1997.

Ricoeur, Paul. *Oneself as Another.* Translated by Kathleen Blamey. Chicago: University of Chicago Press, 1992.

———. *Time and Narrative.* Translated by Kathleen McLaughlin and David Pellauer. 3 vols. Chicago: University of Chicago Press, 1985.

Robinson, Marilynne. *Gilead.* New York: Farrar, 2004.

Rockwood, Kenneth, and James Lindesay. "The Concept of Delirium: Historical Antecedents and Present Meanings." In *Ethical Foundations of Palliative Care for Alzheimer Disease,* edited by Ruth B. Purtilo. Baltimore and London: Johns Hopkins University Press, 2004. 1–8.

Rooke, Constance. "Old Age in Contemporary Fiction." In *Handbook of Humanities and Aging,* edited by Thomas R. Cole, David D Van Tassel, and Robert Kastenbaum. New York: Springer, 1992. 241–57.

Rosemary's Baby. Directed by Roman Polanski. Performed by John Cassavetes, Mia Farrow, Ruth Gordon. Paramount Pictures, 2006.

Rosen, Marjorie. *Popcorn Venus: Women, Movies and the American Dream.* New York: Coward, 1973.

Roth, Philip. *The Human Stain.* New York: Vintage Books, 2001.

Rowe, Kathleen. *The Unruly Woman: Gender and the Genres of Laughter.* Austin: University of Texas Press, 1995.

Royle, Nicholas. *The Uncanny.* New York: Manchester University Press, 2003.

Russell, Catherine. "Mourning the Woman's Film: The Dislocated Spectator of the Company of Strangers." In *Gendering the Nation: Canadian Women's Cinema,* edited by Kay Armatage et al. Toronto: University of Toronto Press, 1999. 212–24.

Sabat, Steven R. "The Self in Dementia." In *The Cambridge Handbook of Age and Ageing,* 332–37.

Salick, Roydon. "'Rampant with Memory': Theme and Technique in *The Stone Angel* and *Frangipani House.*" *Commonwealth Essays and Studies* 14, no. 2 (1992): 98–105.

Schroots, J. J. "Theoretical Developments in the Psychology of Aging." *The Gerontologist* 36, no. 6 (1996): 742–48.

Schwab, Gabriele. *Subjects Without Selves: Transitional Texts in Modern Fiction.* Cambridge, MA: Harvard University Press, 1994.

Schwartz, Hillel. *The Culture of the Copy: Striking Likenesses, Unreasonable Facsimiles.* New York: Zone Books, 1996.

Schwartz, Murray M. Introduction to Schwartz and Woodward, *Memory and Desire,* 1–12.

Schwartz, Murray M., and Kathleen Woodward, eds. *Memory and Desire: Aging-Literature-Psychoanalysis.* Bloomington: Indiana University Press, 1986.

Searching for Debra Winger. Directed by Rosanna Arquette. Lions Gate Films, 2002.

Shields, Carol. *The Stone Diaries.* Toronto: Random House, 1993.

Shuman, Amy. *Other People's Stories: Entitlement Claims and the Critique of Empathy.* Urbana: University of Illinois Press, 2005.

Silverman, Stephen M. "Virginia Madsen: My Botox Confession." *People* (8 May 2007). Sept. 10, 2007: http://www.people.com/people/article/0,,20038279,00.html.

Small, Helen. "The Unquiet Limit: Old Age and Memory in Victorian Narrative." In *Memory and Memorials 1789–1914: Literary and Cultural Perspectives,* edited by Jacqueline M. Labbe and Sally Shuttleworth. London and New York: Routledge, 2000. 60–69.

Smith, Olav Bryant. *Myths of the Self: Narrative Identity and Postmodern Metaphysics.* Lanham, MD: Lexington Books, 2004.

Smith, Paul. *Discerning the Subject.* Minneapolis: University of Minnesota Press, 1988.

Spence, Donald P. *Narrative Truth and Historical Truth: Meaning and Interpretation in Psychoanalysis.* New York: Norton, 1982.

The Straight Story. Directed by David Lynch. Performed by Richard Farnsworth. Alliance Atlantis, 2000.

Stukator, Angela. "Hags, Nags, Witches and Crones: Reframing Age in *The Company of Strangers.*" *Canadian Journal of Film Studies/Revue Canadienne D'Études Cinématographiques* 5, no. 2 (1996): 51–66.

———. "Pictures of Age and Ageing in Cynthia Scott's *The Company of Strangers.*" In *Canada's Best Features: Critical Essays on 15 Canadian Films,* edited by Eugene P. Walz. Amsterdam, Netherlands: Rodopi, 2002. 237–51.

Sunset Boulevard. Directed by Billy Wilder. Performed by William Holden, Gloria Swanson. Paramount Home Video, 1950.

Taylor, Cynthia. "Coming to Terms with the Image of Mother in *The Stone Angel.*" In *New Perspectives on Margaret Laurence: Poetic Narrative, Multiculturalism, and Feminism,* 161–71.

Taylor, Sandra. Letter. *More* (Summer 2007): 18.

Thomas, Clara. "Aging in the Works of Canadian Women Writers." *Canadian Woman Studies/Les Cahiers de la Femme* 5, no. 3 (1984): 45–48.

Todd, Jane Marie. "The Veiled Woman in Freud's 'Das Unheimliche.'" *Signs* 11, no. 3 (1986): 519–28.

Tornstam, Lars. *Gerotranscendence: A Developmental Theory of Positive Aging.* New York: Springer, 2005.

Turner, Bryan S. "Aging and Identity: Some Reflections on the Somatization of the Self." In Featherstone and Wernick, *Images of Aging,* 245–60.

Van Tassel, David D, ed. *Aging, Death, and the Completion of Being.* Philadelphia: University of Pennsylvania Press, 1979.

Venema, Henry Isaac. *Identifying Selfhood: Imagination, Narrative, and Hermeneutics in the Thought of Paul Ricoeur.* Albany: State University of New York Press, 2000.

Venus. Directed by Roger Michell. Performed by Peter O'Toole, Jodi Whittaker. Buena Vista Pictures, 2006.

Vertigo. Directed by Alfred Hitchcock. Performed by Kim Novak, James Stewart. Universal Home Entertainment, 1999.

Waxman, Barbara Frey. *From the Hearth to the Open Road: A Feminist Study of Aging in Contemporary Literature.* New York: Greenwood Press, 1990.

Wernick, Andrew. Introduction to Featherstone and Wernick, *Images of Aging,* 1–28.

Westervelt, Linda A. *Beyond Innocence, Or, the Altersroman in Modern Fiction.* Columbia: University of Missouri Press, 1997.

The Whales of August. Directed by Lindsay Anderson. Performed by Bette Davis, Lillian Gish, Vincent Price. MGM Home Entertainment, 1987.

"What Is Anti-Aging Medicine?" The American Academy of Anti-Aging Medicine. 13 July 2007 http://www.worldhealth.net/p/96,341.html.

Whatever Happened to Baby Jane? Directed by Robert Aldrich. Performed by Bette Davis, Joan Crawford. Warner Home Video, 1962.

Whitehead, Anne. *Trauma Fiction.* Edinburgh: Edinburgh University Press, 2004.

Wolfreys, Julian. *Victorian Hauntings: Spectrality, Gothic, the Uncanny and Literature.* Basingstoke: Palgrave, 2002.

Woodward, Kathleen. *Aging and its Discontents: Freud and Other Fictions.* Bloomington: Indiana University Press, 1991.

———. *At Last, the Real Distinguished Thing: The Late Poems of Eliot, Pound, Stevens, and Williams.* Columbus: The Ohio State University Press, 1980.

———. "Inventing Generational Models: Psychoanalysis, Feminism, Literature." In Woodward, *Figuring Age: Women, Bodies, Generations,* 149–68.

———. "Late Theory, Late Style: Loss and Renewal in Freud and Barthes." In *Aging and Gender in Literature: Studies in Creativity,* edited by Anne M. Wyatt-Brown and Janice Rossen. Charlottesville: University Press of Virginia, 1993. 82–101.

———. "Telling Stories: Aging, Reminiscence, and the Life Review." *Journal of Aging and Identity* 2, no. 3 (1997): 149–63.

———, ed. *Figuring Age: Women, Bodies, Generations.* Bloomington and Indianapolis: Indiana University Press, 1999.

Wyatt-Brown, Anne M. Introduction to *Aging and Gender in Literature: Studies in Creativity,* edited by Anne M. Wyatt-Brown and Janice Rossen. Charlottesville: University of Virginia Press, 1993. 1–15.

York, Lorraine Mary. *Rethinking Women's Collaborative Writing: Power, Difference, Property.* Toronto: University of Toronto Press, 2002.

INDEX